Creative Dream Analysis

Creative Dream Analysis

A GUIDE TO
SELF-DEVELOPMENT

by Reverend Father Gary K. Yamamoto

HARBINGER HOUSE, INC.
TUCSON 1988

ACKNOWLEDGEMENTS

To William Buehler, for his inspiration and guidance
in the field of dreams.

To Sandi, without whose faith and energy
this book would never have been completed.

HARBINGER HOUSE, INC.
Tucson, AZ

Copyright © 1988 by Gary K. Yamamoto
All Rights Reserved
Manufactured in the U.S.A.

This book was set in 10/12 Linotron Trump Mediaeval.

Library of Congress Cataloging-in-Publication Data

Yamamoto, Gary K., 1943 –
Creative dream analysis.
1. Dreams.   I. Title.
BF 1078 Y.36   1988   154.6′34   87-33512
ISBN 0-943173-00-0 (pbk.)

To Laurel

Contents

Introduction

We are all dreamers. The only real difference between us is our ability to recall. On one extreme are those who can recall only an occasional, fleeting image that usually fades away as they awaken. On the other is a living story, full of life and color, with such vivid details that the dreamer must sometimes stop to think if it was really a dream or an actual event in his life. But for most of us, dream recollection falls somewhere between these extremes.

In ancient times, those who were able to interpret the messages of dreams were held in great reverence. If they could interpret their own dreams and predict future events, they were called prophets. If they could interpret the dreams of others, they were believed to be in contact with the Creator and were bestowed with lavish gifts for their powers.

Modern researchers have studied the phenomena of dreams and have made some significant discoveries. Sigmund Freud, the scientific pioneer of dream analysis, believed that there was a sexual or sensual motivation behind all dreams. Carl Jung went deeper and touched on one of the keys of dream analysis. He believed that dreams had a deeper meaning, that they were involved in bringing spiritual direction to a person in a process of unfoldment or evolutionary growth. After Jung, the remainder of the research on dreams has focused primarily on the form of dreaming and not on its content. For example, science has discovered the average person has four or five dream periods each night. Between these periods, the sleeper enters into a state of deep relaxation. The activity of his mind slows down, and his brain waves show the slow, rhythmic pattern associated with deep sleep. Researchers also know that each dream period lasts for about thirty minutes, while the interval between dreams averages about ninety minutes. They also found out that what is called rapid eye movement (REM), which can be easily observed, always accompanies dreaming.

Research has also shown dreams to be an essential part of life. If a person is kept from dreaming for any length of time, his personality will begin to change. Even if other sleep states are experienced, a single night without dreaming will cause nervousness and irritability. The longer the person goes without dreaming, the more irritable he becomes. Finally, if dreaming is prevented for a few days, definite psychological changes in behavior result.

But with all this research on dreams, science has left the symbolic content of dreams alone. Symbols are found to be too complicated, having too many possible meanings. Invariably, they are subject to the personal bias of whoever is providing their meaning.

My interest in dream analysis began with a dream analysis class in 1972 given by Commander William Buehler, United States Navy retired. This was not my first exposure to metaphysics and spirituality. Back in 1954, I began self-defense training in aikido that continued, on and off, for over twenty years. Besides the physical discipline, the training included oriental philosophy and meditation. In 1959, I undertook a year of intensive study in Buddhist theology and considered becoming a Buddhist minister. This was not possible because of my poor comprehension of the Japanese language and the need to learn and master a third language, Sanskrit. But I continued my meditation and studies, which expanded to include other Eastern religions and spirituality. By the middle 1970s, I was teaching classes in palmistry, religion, past-life readings, channeling, healing, massage techniques, awareness training, and many others. I gave readings, mostly in palmistry, tarot, regression analysis, and dream interpretation. In 1984, I was ordained a priest in the Church of Antioch, Malabar Rites. The Church was founded in Antioch (an ancient Syrian city) and moved to Malabar, India. From there, it spread throughout the Far East and eventually into Australia. From Australia, it was brought to the United States. It is not associated with the Roman or Anglican Catholic Churches. Through all this, my interest in dream analysis continued. I took what Commander Buehler provided and began building on it. This book, which records my observations, was started in 1976 and has slowly evolved to its present form.

From many years of study on the subject of dreams, my personal observation has led me to conclude that dreams have a purpose. They provide us with daily guidance. This can be wonderful, except that the language of dreams is symbolic. If we were to ask different people what they thought a symbol meant, their answers would be based on their own backgrounds. Their cultural heritage, religious beliefs, life experiences, education, and present psychological state would all influence their reply. A random sampling from the general public would invariably lead to frustration and failure. The butcher and the vegetarian would probably have conflicting ideas of what the meaning of the symbol "meat" should be. Even if they tried to put their conscious bias aside, their personal ideas and feelings about any given symbol are already a part of their subconscious minds. Results obtained from using Jung's technique of free association, where the tester gives the subject a word and the subject says the first word that comes to mind, will still be colored by personal feelings. Experiments using this method have shown there are only a few symbols that appear to be "archetypal." In order to expand our understanding of a larger number of symbols, a new method had to be found.

The messages of dreams are stored in the deeper subconscious levels of our mind. There are those who are able to tap into those levels. They are called psychics. Of course, psychics are far from infallible. A method to minimize their personal prejudices also had to be developed. After some experimentation, I found that using the synergic energy, or group energy, of several psychics was effective. Using what I will term "group mind," individual traits were minimized, and a clearer meaning for each symbol was obtained. Through an energy bond with several others, sitting in a light meditative state, I channeled the information required to analyze dreams. Although we were able to tap Jung's "universal unconscious," our results were not the elusive archetypal definitions. The definitions obtained were dependent on the level of mind at which humanity was operating.

For the purposes of this book, the definitions we obtained are aimed at individuals who are beginning a personal search for inner growth and self-improvement. The "universal symbols," as I call them, will serve as a guide as we progress through life. It is only a matter of time before we will automatically begin to understand the messages of our dreams, which will provide us guidance and act as signposts of significant moments in our lives. Additionally, the book will reveal how to identify and define our personal symbols. These symbols have a unique meaning to each of us. We will be able to differentiate between the universal and personal symbols and thereby correctly decipher the messages that are being presented.

This book has been written as concisely as possible. Its purpose is to aid in your understanding of the mechanics of dream analysis. But its true value will only be realized after you have recorded your dreams, extracted their messages, and applied these messages to your life. I hope you will find it a tool to assist you in handling the problems of life and in guiding you in discovering and fulfilling your life's mission.

I

Sleep:
The Wasted One-Third
of Our Life?

During a session of a dream analysis class that I was teaching, I asked if anyone had a dream to share that could be used as an example. One of the students, a woman, raised her hand to volunteer.

● I don't understand this, but I had a dream where I was walking down a dusty country road, one with a lot of holes and rocks. I met a man who was beating on a cat with his hands. The cat was a calico, and looked terrible, just horribly beaten. As I watched what was happening, I felt no sorrow. There was an empty, hollow feeling in my stomach. I turned away from this gross scene and continued down the road until I came upon a paved road. It was a regular road, except that there were a lot of rods sticking up from the black stuff [asphalt]. I thought that this would be dangerous for anyone passing this way. I saw a road crew sitting on the side of the road. I went over to them and asked when they were going to repave this road. They said that they had no idea. I explained to them how dangerous this was and they agreed, but they still didn't do anything. I finally got upset and yelled, "What the hell are you waiting for?" One of them smiled and replied, "The boss says that if we repair the road too soon, there will be no more excitement." I then woke up.

"How did you feel about the dream?" I asked.
"Well, I think I felt frustrated."
"Do you remember any colors?"
"The calico cat, and when I was looking at the cat it was like looking through a veil, and the veil was yellow. Oh! There was also a red stop sign on the country road where it met the paved road."

I thought about the dream for a few moments and gave her the following interpretation:

> The cat symbolizes your relationship with a man, either your husband, or even a boyfriend. The horrible condition of the cat tells me there has been a lot of mental and maybe even physical abuse between you. It's very difficult for both of you, and there is no real relationship. You've probably thought of ending this relationship and walking out on him many times before. The black road means you don't have a clear idea how to do it yet. The rods sticking up on the road symbolize unknown dangers in your path. You're afraid that things might become very difficult for you if you were on your own. The fear that you have is really created in your mind. This is not to say that the problems themselves are not real, but you've created an unreasonable fear of the situation.
>
> The road crew symbolizes help for you whenever you really need it. When the boss said they kept the rods because they needed excitement, it indicates you want to continue this relationship. Most of us are creatures of habit and rarely venture into new things. You are now standing at one of the major crossroads of your life. You have to make a decision, if not now, soon. Once that decision is made, things will appear to take care of themselves. Maintaining this relationship will only be more of the same. Ending it will cause many changes, and things will be easier than you think.

As I finished the analysis, I noticed that the woman had been strongly affected. She had become flushed, and there was a far-away look in her eyes. She began telling us how difficult her relationship was with her husband. She had tried leaving him before, but consideration for her children always made her return to him. The tears began to flow as she expressed her frustration with the situation. "How am I going to correct my problem? I can't afford to do anything. How can I? I can't afford to! There's no way to do it!"

"Listen to your dream," I advised her. "It's describing both the problem and the solution. You have to make a decision, regardless of how difficult it appears to be. If you say that it's impossible, then there is no hope. There are no more possibilities open to you. But if you try, it may be possible for something new to come into your life. It won't be easy, but help will be there as long as you don't quit."

Still crying, she nodded and said that she would try.

Many months later, I found out the results of my interpretation. She had taken action. She seemed a new woman, prettier and definitely more alive. She said that she had found a job and moved out of her house. She had met another man, one with whom she was establishing a good relationship. As I talked to her, she was bubbling with excitement and said she wanted to know only one more thing—"There is this dream that I have over and over. . . ."

I felt quite gratified to see someone taking care of a problem based on the guidance provided by their dreams. Most people are not really interested in solving their problems. While they may show the greatest interest in having their dreams analyzed and having their problems revealed, few have either the will or the energy to do something about them. Identifying a problem is simple. Correcting it is where the real work begins.

The Purpose of Dreams

Many of us consider sleep a waste of time, an inconvenience that interferes with the more important things of life. We go to bed at odd hours, often not getting enough sleep. Or we push ourselves, sometimes to the point of exhaustion, before finally allowing the body to rest. We need tranquilizers to put us to sleep, followed by stimulants to get us going again. Is it any wonder that we never seem to get sufficient rest? And our dreams receive almost no attention at all. We feel that dreams are simple, natural phenomena having little or no significance, or they are just another interesting curiosity of life.

In discussing dream analysis, our initial considerations are the significance of dreams and their interpretation. To understand these, we must look into the psychological mechanism that drives people's lives. Carl Jung thought that people were tied together through a common and vast intelligence called the "collective unconscious." A more descriptive term for our purposes is "universal intelligence," which is the storehouse of the total experience and knowledge of all mankind. Though this unlimited source of information seems to lie just beyond our ability to recognize and use it, it is actually providing constant guidance. Messages from the universal intelligence flow in a continuous stream, guiding each of us from moment to moment. Some people call this their conscience or say that they hear a "small voice" inside their mind. We will call our ability to communicate with the universal intelligence our "inner intelligence."

Unfortunately, most of us are unable to hear these messages during the day. We are too occupied with our usual daily routine. Work, family life, domestic chores, and other activities, such as sports, listening to music, socializing, reading, or even just thinking, continually involve us. Not that there is anything wrong with these, for they comprise the bulk of mainstream behavior. But inside each of us is the gnawing awareness that there is more to life. We have an inborn need to touch this greater level of intelligence. If we fail to do so, the messages will simply drift past and never be heard. Fortunately, there is a regular period when the continuous movement of our mind and body stops and we can receive the messages from the universal intelligence. This is when we sleep. And with sleep, we dream.

During sleep, our inner intelligence freely communicates with the universal intelligence. Our dreams become powerful tools for solving our problems and helping in our self-growth.

But we must learn to interpret and understand the messages of this communication, which are revealed through our dreams. For example, a dream may reenact a situation that is causing a problem and present a solution. While there are many ways to solve any problem, the solution provided in our dream will probably be a very practical one, one that we can apply immediately. As we make changes in our lives, our dreams will change accordingly. Each moment-by-moment decision will cause our messages to adapt and change appropriately. No problem is ever too great to be handled by our dreams. Each problem is given a turn, depending on its relative urgency. Small problems may receive only a brief review, while the severe ones will be reviewed periodically, even nightly. By learning to record and analyze our dreams, we can use them to solve these problems.

We may have the same dream over and over, although the symbols of the dream may change slightly. We will continue to have this dream until we acknowledge its message and act on the solution it is giving us or when the problem fades into insignificance by other more pressing situations. Herein lies the value of being able to analyze our dreams: we can immediately recognize a problem and then follow through with an appropriate action. Greek philosophers long ago stressed the importance of self-knowledge as the path to wisdom. Our dreams can be the medium through which we achieve insight into ourselves. Constructive use of the knowledge gained will result in change, growth, and eventually wisdom. This process occurs as a natural consequence of our evolution.

2
Types of Dreams

We all experience many different dreams every night. As each dream weaves its complex pattern, we can appreciate the infinite variety of dreams that evolve. There are prophetic dreams, inspirational dreams, wishful dreams, dreams on the problems of the day, and nightmares. Although our dreams appear to be different, they all have one thing in common. *All our dreams can help us solve our problems.* Every problem we have is a candidate for our dreams to solve. Although all dreams have the same function, they can be categorized into three types: dreams to clear everyday problems, spiritual guidance dreams, and psychic dreams. Of these three, the former is the most common. Most dreams work on the problems of the physical world, or what we call everyday life.

None of us is spared from life's onslaught of problems. There are office problems, family problems, financial problems, problems with relatives—the list is almost endless. As if these were not enough, we are also called upon to make decisions, choices of great consequence to ourselves. Is this the right place to work or should I find another job? Should I stay in this relationship? What can I do to resolve the problem between my spouse and myself? The difficulty of decision-making and our inability often to make the correct choices at the right time create stress. This is the plague of modern living. Psychologists have found that stress is the major cause of many of man's physical and mental ailments.

Of course, there are always those who say that they never take their problems home from the office and claim they are able to forget everything as soon as they walk out the door. However, these individuals are probably fooling themselves. Rarely does a single incident result in a major problem. Stress is created over time, after days, weeks, and even years of the repetition of events. A problem during the day may trigger the release of a vast store of memories of similar incidents from our past. Now, instead of having a single problem, we are confronted with many. The emotions from our memories are restimulated and compound each other. When we finally walk out of the office and head home, these problems will not simply disappear. They linger on and on, resulting in an ever-rising level of stress. Unless this constant buildup is stopped, it may become impossible for us to maintain a proper psychological balance.

Physical/Emotional Clearance Dreams

When we finally retire and lie in bed at the end of the day, it is easy for our body to relax and be ready for sleep. The mind, however, is still mulling over what happened during the day. But resting the mind is so important that a deeper level of mind takes over. This deeper level of mind, or our inner intelligence, is a vast, untapped reservoir of wisdom and creativity. Communication flows out of our inner intelligence through the dynamic movement of symbols, which make up the language of dreams.

As soon as we fall asleep, dreams are begun by our inner intelligence. Our most pressing problem, including the events leading up to it and its ramifications, will be recreated symbolically. Our inner intelligence then begins to formulate a solution. Owing to the nature of the symbolic language, the solution may not appear to be reasonable or logical to our analytical minds. For example, suppose our problem is with a tyrannical boss. In our dreams, we may shoot him with a gun. This solution is neither reasonable nor logical, but it is a solution, one that will satisfy the mind and allow it to once again attempt to join the body and get some rest. Usually, however, additional problems are encountered, and rest is not yet possible. Our inner intelligence will recreate another problem and provide yet another solution. Because these dreams solve problems in the physical or material world that result in an emotional reaction, we shall call them "physical/emotional clearance" dreams, or more simply, "clearance" dreams. This clearance process usually continues for about a half an hour until all problems encountered are solved. When completed, both mind and body can rest simultaneously.

A period of deep rest follows for approximately an hour and a half. Both the mind and body are able to use this period for complete rejuvenation. The mind then rises to a level of greater consciousness and continues the process of clearance through a new set of dreams. Again our inner intelligence symbolically recreates our problems and provides probable solutions. This continues until this second phase of problem resolution is completed and rest is again possible. This process of recreating and resolving problems usually occurs during four major dream periods each night. During each succeeding period, we become more consciously aware of the problem being solved.

Sometimes our problems are so overwhelming, having so much emotion tied to them, that our inner intelligence is unable to release the charge. When this happens, we may spend the night tossing and turning. Our mind is in a state of constant motion, trying to resolve the problem. As a result, we may not get enough rest and get up feeling even more tired than when we went to bed. The dream we remember the next morning will be another re-creation of our problem. An example of this kind of dream is related below:

> ◑ In this dream, I spent a lot of time adjusting knobs and dials. There seemed to be an endless number of these, and I knew that they had to be adjusted correctly so that I could communicate. I had no idea who I was trying to communicate with, only that I had to. There was a lot of

urgency to complete what I was doing. It seems that I would almost get it, only to have the communications distorted. I got up feeling beat.

The person relating this dream had just built a microwave television receiver. He then spent the rest of the evening trying to get the system to function. No matter what he did, it failed to work properly. Finally, tired and frustrated, he retired for the night. The dream he remembered the next morning accurately identified his inability to communicate with his receiver. It also depicted his frustration of not being able to complete his project.

Because the dream remembered when waking is usually the last dream of the night, this clearance dream shows how a seemingly normal event can cause great inner turmoil. The simple act of not being able to properly adjust his new receiver bothered this man so much that he spent most of his night on this problem. There is nothing wrong in remembering a clearance dream. It is our built-in stress-reduction mechanism that enables us to maintain some level of stability. But if we continually wake up feeling tired, remembering the same or similar clearance dreams, then it is time for us to do something. The problems of life are troubling us much more than we would like to believe. We need to resolve them as soon as possible. The pent-up emotional charge has to be removed so we can gain more rest during the night. (One method for accomplishing this is covered in detail in chapter 7.) If nothing is done, our stress level will remain high, ultimately resulting in some sort of physical or emotional breakdown.

There are certain incidents that make remembering a clearance dream more likely. For example, if someone wakes us when we nap in the afternoon, any dream we remember will probably be a clearance one. When an alarm wakes us before we are ready to get up, the dream cycle will be shortened, and we will probably be in the middle of a clearance dream.

A good night's sleep will usually remove much of the emotional charge attached to our problems. We should get up feeling refreshed, free of the burdens created by our problems. Unfortunately, this blissful state does not last very long. Shortly after waking, similar incidents once again remind us of our problems. The problems reenter our conscious mind and trigger our memories of similar problems in the past. The emotional charge attached to these problems is also stimulated. New life has been given to all the problems our inner intelligence had so diligently removed. The problems will once again have the emotional energy to build stress and interfere with our well-being. Fortunately, when night comes and we once again fall asleep, our inner intelligence will unfailingly work to release our problems. As all physicians know, by morning we will feel better. This is not a special gift given to a chosen few. It is a natural process, one that our body and mind attempt to repeat each night.

If we find ourselves in a stress cycle, we can break it. To do so, we must first recognize the problem being described by our dream. Then, we need to take some corrective action to change our present situation. If nothing is done, we will remain in a vicious cycle. Over and over, the problem will reoccur, and we may spend a major portion of our life trying to resolve it. This kind of unresolved problem will be expressed as a repeating dream, one that we may have during our whole life. The following illustrates a repeating dream:

> ◗ I have had this dream every so often for over thirty years. I am living alone on a farm. My legs are crippled, and it's impossible for me to walk. I want to plant a garden, because I'll get a prize if I do it. Somehow I know that the prize is a rock or a stone. To get around, I ride a donkey. It's hard to do anything because I have to fight with the donkey to make it go. I have no one to help me. I ask for help from some strangers who pass, but they only smile politely. I get so frustrated and begin to curse myself. I'm so upset that I go to my room, lock the door, and sit on the floor. I sit there for a long time, staring at the wall.

The actual method for analysis is covered in chapter 5. For now, it is sufficient that we understand the message of the dream. This person's goal is to find or obtain harmony (stone) within himself. He has been given all that is required to attain this harmony (farm), *but it requires work*. He is stubborn (donkey), which keeps him from listening to those who would advise him. He seeks advice from those who are themselves lost (strangers). He knows that there is something missing in his life (frustration and cursing). The solution to his problem is to go within himself (room) and meditate (staring at the wall) or analyze his situation.

When this interpretation was provided, the man immediately recognized the accuracy of the dream. He realized that this dream had been pointing out the great frustration he had with life. Inwardly, he knew that something was wrong with his life. Outwardly, he could not put his frustration into words. He could only ask "How?" How was he going to do what he had to do? How was he going to meditate and solve his problems? These questions are asked by many who have their dreams interpreted. They want a formula, some kind of step-by-step procedure. But the dream has given them a solution—to become quiet and to go within themselves. The "how" will come when we take the first step, doing or at least trying to do what has been suggested by our dream.

Consider an athlete who wants to improve his performance. For him, there is only one method—training. The coach does not tell him how to move his arms or legs. It is assumed that he knows how to walk and run. The coach makes him practice. As the coach watches him train, he will notice what the athlete is doing wrong. He will give him a few words of advice. It will be short and simple, like "Relax your arms!" or "Your stride is too long!" Then it is back to more training. But the athlete will consciously and subconsciously remember the coach's advice. As he practices and adjusts his movements, his performance will begin to show the results of his efforts. This is the body's biofeedback mechanism at work. Anything that improves performance will be automatically adopted by the body as its new norm. If something decreases performance, the body will reject it, providing that conscious thoughts are not interfering with the process.

In the same way, our lives are a moving, dynamic process, changing from moment to moment. The same problem has to be handled differently by different individuals. There is no formula or procedure that works for everyone. But our inner intelligence knows what we have to do in our present situation. So we do what we think is best. Whatever we do will be better than doing nothing. If we choose the right solution, the problem will fade away, and our dreams on the subject will end. If our solution does not work or only partially works, our dreams will change to compensate for our efforts. They will indicate what is happening now and recommend the next step. Remember that each moment in time is the beginning of the rest of your life. Each moment requires a new decision that forms the foundation for all future decisions. Fortunately, our dreams are adaptable, moving and changing in step with anything we choose to do.

The actual mechanics of the relationship between dreams and the resultant changes are fairly straightforward. Every decision we make, every action we take is recorded by our inner intelligence. Based on this everchanging input, our inner intelligence creates new dreams. These dreams identify any new pitfalls, provide possible solutions, and may reveal the outcomes of the paths being followed. Although there are an infinite number of possible directions we can take, our dreams select only a few. We only have to follow their guidance. Fortunately, dreams are not influenced by anything we say or anything we promise to do tomorrow or sometime in the future. Dreams only recognize what is happening relative to past actions, and the messages of dreams are based on this reality.

As we make changes in some area of our lives, subtle changes also occur in many other areas. There will be physical changes in either our body or environment. As physical changes come into being, more changes will occur in the subconscious levels of our mind. Changes in our subconscious beliefs will change the dreams we remember when waking. *New actions, guided by our dreams, result in physical changes. These cause psychological changes, which in turn change our dreams*. This cyclic process continues as long as we are willing to take action to resolve the problems identified by our dreams. Automatically, we move closer to a condition of more vitality and awareness. Clinging to old beliefs and habits nullifies this process and keeps us in a state of stress and constant worry. Until we complete the necessary changes in our life, we must resist the temptation to slide into old and more comfortable patterns.

Spiritual Guidance Dreams

As changes occur in our lives, clearance dreams will no longer be our last dreams of the night. Instead, our dreams will evolve into what we will call spiritual guidance dreams. These provide us with the necessary guidance for our spiritual evolvement. They reveal the missing bits and pieces of our past that we have overlooked or forgotten. We must reflect on our past mistakes, and then do something to correct them. But in our fast-paced, modern society, there never seems to be enough time for us to reflect on our lives, much less think about spiritual growth. Most of us are primarily concerned with maintaining or increasing our position in society. Our goals are centered around developing our personal identity, security, power, and sexuality. There never seems to be time for real introspection. Jesus directed us where to look, saying that the kingdom of heaven was within us. Spiritual guidance dreams reveal the great wealth of wisdom we hold within and represent the highest ideals of mankind, touching the intelligence of our actions, the significance and direction of our lives, and the morality of all our relationships. An example of this type of dream is given below:

> ◗ I dreamt of going into an open field. There were many trees around me, and the grass was soft and green. I sat there watching the birds for a while. I thought, "I bet that I can fly." So I got up and ran across the field. About half way across the field, I jumped and held my hands out and rose quickly into the air. "This is really neat," I thought. "There's nothing to this flying stuff." I was soaring higher and higher, really enjoying the view. As I continued to fly, I thought about how I was able to do this, especially how I could remain in the air without any effort on my part. It suddenly flashed into my head that I shouldn't be able to do this, and I began to lose altitude. When I did land, I would run again and jump, only to fly a short distance and return back to the ground. "This is foolish," I thought. "I know less now than when I began." I then woke up.

This type of dream is easy to recognize. Its "language" is highly symbolic, and what happens is illogical or out of the ordinary. The symbols in a spiritual guidance dream will be referred to as universal symbols. They have a deep meaning that has evolved from the combined consciousness of mankind. Within these symbols lies the message that the dream is trying to convey. (A dictionary of these symbols is at the back of this book.)

The purpose of a spiritual guidance dream is to help us in the fulfillment of our life's mission. Although we usually have little conscious awareness of this mission, the deeper levels of our mind are completely in tune with it. A dream serves as a link between the conscious and the deeper levels of our mind, allowing a form of communication between the two. In sleep, after all necessary clearance dreams have been completed, our dreams can then be directed spiritually. If we are not heading in the right direction, our dreams will provide suggestions. Many different scenes and situations will be created giving us the same message. Even nightmares may be experienced to shake us out of our growing complacency.

Eventually the drive may become so strong that we cannot continue on our present path. Inwardly, our whole life comes to a standstill. Outwardly, our personality begins to change. Our mind begins to churn as we search for a solution to this inner turmoil and frustration. Our reaction to this search is very predictable—we blame others for our problems or the situations in which we find ourself. We may become more involved with outer distractions. We may use alcohol or drugs to silence what our inner voice is trying to say to us. Smoking or overeating may be used to numb our feelings. Sports may become important, tiring our body and mind. Sexual encounters may be used to divert our attention from inner movements to outer desires. Greater importance may be placed on work, hobbies, and social events, as they serve to distract and prevent us from facing the real drive that comes from within. At best, these activities only provide temporary answers and avoid the more important inner issues. In time, all these activities will lead to a total frustration with life. "Is this all there is to life?" is the cry that we have all heard or repeated quite often.

What is the answer to this cry? We can seldom find it in the "normal" people that we meet. They, too, are searching, frustrated, and missing the essence of life. But history has recorded a few rare occasions when someone has risen above the ordinary concerns of humanity. These were and still are the master teachers of mankind. Jesus said to seek the kingdom of heaven which is within. Krishna said that the limitations of man are in his mind, created by himself. Buddha said that the world is one of suffering and that the path to end suffering is to search within the silence and practice right actions, right thoughts, and right deeds. So our answers are within ourselves, within the recesses of our subconscious minds. The subconscious is usually out of the reach of the conscious mind. The vast complex of memories and drives that make up the subconscious moves and acts as if it were completely independent. Conscious thought has little effect on it. Those who have been trying to lose weight or quit smoking know this all too well. Regardless of how many good reasons the conscious mind can think of, no matter how many great resolutions and public statements are made, the results are usually the same. The subconscious mind does not believe any of our reasons, resolutions, or statements, and we remain overweight or continue smoking. Fortunately, this powerful level of mind can be reached. As night comes and we fall asleep, a bridge is created between our outer consciousness and our inner intelligence. This bridge is our dreams.

Psychic Dreams

Psychic dreams receive a lot of attention from the public. These dreams are the natural outgrowth of spiritual guidance dreams. During the many dreams of a night, there are occasions when a dream may pierce the time/space barrier creating a psychic dream. The purpose of psychic dreams is to help us prepare for a probable event, usually in the future. The following is quite typical of a psychic dream:

> ◐ There were many people on the beach in my dream. Many of them were swimming. The ocean was really blue and the white caps were large, and there were many seagulls flying. Out in the deep was a girl swimming. Sud-

denly, she began frantically waving her arms and calling for help. I yelled for someone in the water to go to her aid, but no one heard me. I ran to the water, and everything slowed down, as if in slow motion. No matter how hard I tried, I couldn't reach her. I woke up. I was in a cold sweat and felt very bad. Then, I had difficulty going back to sleep.

This dreamer had touched the realm where the laws of time and space no longer apply, which enabled him to witness a highly probable event. This type of dream is truly fantastic. Imagine how wonderful it would be to be able to see what is about to happen long before it does. There is, however, one small problem. It is usually difficult to determine the exact place where this event will happen and nearly impossible to determine the exact date and time. In the example given, the dreamer also saw the futility of trying to stop the event. This doesn't mean that it's impossible, it can be done. But the probability of changing the outcome is slim, and the event will most likely happen just as the dreamer saw it. If the dreamer happened to be on the very beach that the dream depicted and at the time when the girl was having difficulty swimming, it is possible that he could save her. In this case, the dreamer did find himself at the beach he had seen in his dream. On the third day of his vacation, he heard of a near drowning that had occurred that morning. When he went down to the beach, the commotion was over. The ambulance and rescue people had already left the scene. He had a sickening feeling in his stomach. His inability to help the girl in the dream probably meant that he was not destined to help save her life in reality.

In the case of a larger occurrence, such as a plane crash, there is little that we could do to prevent the crash. The airlines would never stop any of their flights based on what they would call our "bad dreams." Nor is there anything that we could do to physically stop the plane from falling. We might be able to get ourselves out of the way of the crash or inform those who might be willing to listen to our advice on the impending accident. Removing ourselves from danger is usually the message of the dream.

Dreams are the door through which many people encounter their first psychic or prophetic experience. These dream experiences have also been called ESP, or extrasensory perception. ESP is not a talent given to a chosen few. It is a natural part of each of us. It simply lies dormant, awaiting the moment of awakening. Those who have awakened this ability and actively use it are called psychics.

A more common form of a psychic dream is one in which a relative or a friend is in trouble. These dreams are triggered by an emotional tie between the person in trouble and ourselves. Events that trigger heavy emotions include death, illness, divorce, being fired, and being in an accident. When one of these occurs, the person in trouble will have a very strong emotional, even hysterical, reaction to the situation. This strong signal will be put out into the universe in the same manner that a radio transmitter transmits. Those of us who have an emotional tie to the person are more likely to "tune in" and receive this signal in our dreams. This doesn't mean that more mundane signals will be missed. They are also received, but we are more likely to remember the more emotional ones when we awaken. We are all familiar with the stories of parents whose sons were hurt or killed during a war. Many have told of having dreams in which their sons were dying or injured. These dreams usually occurred at the same moment as the actual event. This is another way in which our inner consciousness tries to help us by preparing us for a future, traumatic event. The following story was provided by a person who experienced a stressful event:

◗ I had been working at a new communications facility on the North West Cape of Australia. In the morning, another person and I got into a vehicle and took a trip, something to break the monotony of work. We were heading across the desert to the swamps to collect shells. As we were driving on the road, we took a wrong turn and got lost in the desert. Driving through the sand, it wasn't long before we got stuck. It was very, very hot. There were no trees and no shade. We had not brought any food or water with us. All we had was a single can of soda pop, which we drank quickly. As the day wore on, the blazing sun got hotter and hotter. There was some water available in the windshield washer container, but we didn't want to drink it. When our thirst became unbearable, we used the water to wet our mouths. When night finally came, it became cold. We thought of leaving the vehicle and getting some exercise to warm up, but we could hear the dingos, or wild dogs, outside. So we huddled in the vehicle under a few sheets of newspaper to wait out the night. In the morning, we got up very early to start walking. We walked for some time before we were finally found by those who were looking for us. The real story begins when I received a letter from my parents a few days later. They were worried about me. It seems that they both had dreams of my being in trouble on the same night. I looked at the date of their dreams and saw that they had occurred at almost the same time that my friend and I were stuck in the desert.

If anything serious had happened to this person, his parents would have been prepared. Their dreams would have given them a hint of what might be happening to their son. They may not have known the whole story or the final outcome, but inwardly, they would have been prepared.

Psychic Dreams of the Past

Not all psychic dreams are of future events. A psychic dream may also depict an event from a time long past or a place long forgotten. Wondering about what caused something to happen, planning a trip, trying to imagine what the past was really like can trigger this type of psychic dream. Reading a book on ancient Egypt or attending an exhibit of the treasures of Tutankhamen may cause you to dream of ancient Egypt. A dream of ancient Greece might be triggered by seeing a movie on Helen of Troy or by watching the Olympics on television. The following dream was experienced by a person studying the pyramids of Egypt:

❂ I had the strangest dream. It was in ancient Egypt. I knew it was back then since the pyramids were in the process of being built. I must have been rich or a member of the royal family because I had a large home and several servants. There were many rich carpets on the floor, and everything was made of stone. The buildings were cold, which is surprising for Egypt. There was a large party, with several musicians and some dancers. There was one dancer who was really beautiful. She was so sensual when she danced that I had to make love to her. I sent everyone else away and took her to my bedroom. There she danced for me, and we made love. It was unbelievable. It was so real that I actually felt her. I mean, she was there, just like I was there. When I finally woke up, I sat on my bed for a long time thinking about my dream. Even now, it seems more real than a lot of things that have happened to me in real life.

This is another typical psychic dream that transcended the limits of time. The strong feeling that the events of the dream are real is commonly experienced by those who report having this kind of psychic dream.

In some cases, we may not remember having our dream upon awakening. At some later date, however, we may experience déjà vu, knowing that we have either been to or seen a place before. This is quite common and is usually accompanied by a feeling of excitement and a tingling sensation through the spine and body. The chills are a definite confirmation of the event. The following is an example of a déjà vu experience resulting from a dream:

◗ I was taking a vacation in California. It was my first trip into the state, and I was just driving up to Yosemite National Park. I stopped at the city of Merced and found a motel somewhere in the outskirts of the city. There I got a room, took a bath, and stepped out to get some dinner. As I walked to the end of the motel, I thought I knew what was around the building. I knew that there was a courtyard with a flagpole in the middle. As I made the turn, there was that same courtyard with the flagpole. Seeing this made me feel energetic. I also knew that across the street was a good restaurant that was hidden from the road by a row of pine trees. Somehow I also knew that they specialized in trout. As I crossed the street, there was the hedge of pine, partially hiding a restaurant. As I walked up, it was the same restaurant I had seen before. I walked in, and the waitress gave me the menu and said that the specialty of the house was fresh trout. It was a good thing that I was sitting since it really blew my mind.

This was the first major déjà vu experience for this person. He has had many similar experiences since then, but this one opened his eyes. The probable trigger was the fact that this was his first trip to California. His excitement and anticipation probably precipitated this psychic dream. The dream was not remembered until he was at the actual place the dream had previewed. Only then were the gates of his memory opened, and he realized that he had been there before. Ordinary events may also trigger this type of experience. Many people have related such experiences, which may be as simple as seeing a hidden valley in a national park or sitting in a soccer field and suddenly knowing that they have been there before.

Even with all these different types of psychic dreams, their purpose remains the same. They warn us of and prepare us for change. Every significant event in our lives will be previewed by at least one psychic dream. In the case of a traumatic or exciting event, our dreams may repeat the same theme continually over a period of weeks or even months. It is unlikely, however, that we can change the outcome of the events predicted by these dreams. The primary purpose of psychic dreams is to prepare us for these events.

3

Recording Dreams

Recording your dreams is the first step in dream analysis. Begin by keeping a pen and notebook next to your bed. An easily accessible light switch is helpful if you get up when it is still dark. (While fumbling for a light switch, the details of a dream may fade away before you can write them down.) You should also recall any feelings experienced during the dream. Record these in the margin, next to the appropriate text. The following is an example from a dream "diary":

happy
excited

proud

sorry
for horse

◗ In my dream, I was riding a horse, a white horse. The horse and I galloped across a farm and began to climb this hill. The hill was pretty steep, but my horse had no trouble getting to the top. I really felt good as the wind blew through my hair and on my face. When I reached the top, I looked around and thought the view was beautiful. I turned the horse around and headed down to the barn. When I looked at the horse, it just wasn't the same horse. It looked tired and didn't want to run. I urged the horse on, and with much straining we were able to return to the base of the hill. We slowly began to climb back up, but I could see that there was little left in him. I *crying*   wanted to give up and thought that we could be just as happy if we just walked around the base of the hill. I felt very strange inside.

Recording a dream in this manner makes it easy to see how your emotions relate to the story. It provides more depth to the message that the dream is revealing.

Remembering the Dream

Some of us have difficulty remembering our dreams. We may either have no recollection at all or are only able to recall a few vague, fleeting moments. Until now, there probably was no real reason to try to remember our dreams. However, once we decide that we want to learn from our dreams and make an effort to do so, we will begin to remember many dreams.

One of the most common causes of the inability to recall dreams is the lack of sleep. Trying to get more out of life by spending less time sleeping seems to be approaching a national mania. For those of us who are pursuing this type of lifestyle, getting up in the morning can be a difficult and sometimes agonizing event. Only the sound of the alarm clock and the driving need to be somewhere get us going. Physical exhaustion, emotional drain, and mental drowsiness make dream recollection almost impossible. Our solution may be as simple as getting more sleep.

Another aid is to get up without an alarm clock. While retirees, the wealthy, and the self-employed seem to have a definite edge, anyone can rise without a jarring alarm. This does not mean we should sleep as long as possible either. Sleeping past the "necessary" amount also impedes dream recollection since the additional time is usually spent in a fitful sleep. It is best to go to sleep at a reasonable hour with a waking time in mind. Within our mind is a mental clock that keeps accurate time, even while we sleep. Mentally state, "I want to get up at 6:30." This will set our mental clock. Experience shows that most of us are able to rise within a few minutes of the desired time. Skeptics of this method should note how easy it is to get up early when looking forward to an event, such as going fishing. Under such positive conditions, we can usually wake up easily before it is time and still feel wide awake. But for those who insist that waking without an alarm is impossible, having the music from a clock radio may prove to be a beneficial alternative.

It is also interesting to note here that anyone who relies on such drugs as sleeping pills, tranquilizers, or alcohol does not receive any real sleep. Instead of inducing natural sleep, these drugs render a person completely unconscious. Natural sleep allows only the conscious mind to become quiet and rest. Drugs, on the other hand, knock out the entire mind. The sleeper is no longer resting. He is simply out cold, totally oblivious to everything. Drugged sleepers do not exhibit any REM, which always accompanies dreaming. Thus, there can be no bridge between the conscious mind and the inner intelligence since the drugs have incapacitated the mind. Under these conditions, it is little wonder that those taking sleeping pills wake in the morning feeling even more tired than when they went to bed. They are actually suffering from sleep deprivation. Then they have to use another drug to get going in the morning so they take a stimulant, such as caffeine or some kind of pill. Over time, sleep and dream deprivation may have severe psychological and behavioral effects.

But suppose we may receive enough sleep but are still unable to recall our dreams. A psychological block may be preventing recall. While there are many methods to remove these blocks, the following has proven successful with a lot of people.

1. Get a glass of water just before going to bed. Be sure it has a cover. It's disturbing to find that something has shared the water during the night and is now floating on top of it.

2. Say out loud, "I will drink half of the water now to prepare me to remember my dreams. In the morning, when I drink the rest of this water, I will remember my dreams."

3. Drink half the water in the glass. Put the cover on the glass and set it in some convenient place near your bed.

4. Go to sleep.

5. When waking the next morning, say out loud with emotion, "Upon drinking this glass of water, I will remember my dreams!"

6. Drink the rest of the water. (Steps 5 and 6 are omitted if a dream is recalled.)

Drinking the rest of the water in the morning will usually trigger the recollection of a dream. If this doesn't happen at first, we must not give up. Sometimes, nightly repetition may be required before we obtain results. With so much to be gained through dream recollection and analysis, our efforts are definitely worthwhile. Occasionally, we may not remember our dreams until later in the day. It is imperative that we stop whatever we are doing to record them—even if we are in the middle of a bath or driving down the street. This is especially important if we are remembering our first dream after years of minimal recall. Unless we do this, our newly acquired ability may fade away once again, which will make any future attempts even more difficult. Not recording a dream is interpreted by our subconscious as lack of interest; not remembering is assumed to be what we really want, and our subconscious mind will respond accordingly.

There is one method of stimulating dream recall that has never failed. This method requires the aid of an assistant, someone who is willing to stay up all night and watch us while we sleep. (We can offer to trade this act with a friend or partner who is also interested in learning from their dreams.) Our assistant is responsible for waking us right after we have completed a dream. When we dream, our eyes move and twitch behind our closed lids (the rapid eye movement, or REM, already mentioned). Our partner should wait until the REM stops and then gently awaken us. We will remember the dream we have just completed. Our assistant can further help by questioning us and writing down what we remember. If there are any areas that need clarification, he can further prompt us until as much detail as possible has been recorded. Naturally, this method should not be used on a regular basis. Being awakened right after a dream will interfere with our sleep, and we may not obtain the necessary rest we need. But if we must rely on this technique, it is best to be awakened after the last REM period, which is usually early in the morning. This will result in the least interference with our sleep and allow us to remember the last and most significant dream of the night.

Recording the Dream

Each dream should be dated in our notebook. I recommend skipping every other line to allow for later additions when more details are remembered. Once recorded, our dreams cannot be forgotten, and we can work on their analysis whenever time permits. We should also keep the analysis in our dream book. Together, they serve as our personal diary, keeping track of our dreams and whatever progress we have made.

There is another important reason for maintaining this book. Once a problem has been identified and written down, our inner intelligence will demand action. Some change in our life is forthcoming. At this point, we must remember to *keep a positive attitude*. The direction of change will be greatly influenced by our attitude. A negative attitude will create negative results. Conversely, a positive attitude will create a positive outcome, although it may not be the one we expect.

Dreams are dynamic, changing as we change. Because it is such a dynamic tool, a dream is only significant for a short period after it is experienced. Dreams that are several years old, or even a few months old, probably have little or no validity today. There is one exception, however—the repeating dream. *Repeating dreams are very significant*. They are reminding us that we have a long-standing, unresolved problem from the past. These dreams are the first ones we should analyze and work on. Solving the problems that manifest themselves in repeating dreams will result in the most significant changes in the quality of our lives.

4
Symbols

S ymbols are a universal form of communication, the value of which has long been recognized. The messages of a successful hunt that early man scratched on the walls of caves can still be read and understood today. Confucius knew the power of a symbol when he said a picture is worth a thousand words. Jesus also recognized the value of symbols when he spoke to the masses. His messages were always in the form of parables, or stories that incorporate symbols. By using a symbolic language, Jesus was able to present deep conceptual truths to people from all walks of life. Their different backgrounds did not matter. Fishermen, farmers, priests, and tax collectors could understand him, thus demonstrating the ease of symbolic communication. When each of us reads a parable, we extract a universal principle. Based on our own experiences, we also receive a personal message. This personal message is always changing, changing to the same degree that we change. Each step in our evolution changes the message and reveals more wisdom.

The Wizard of Oz and Alice in Wonderland are excellent examples of symbolic stories. When we were introduced to these as children, we enjoyed them as good stories. We knew we liked them, but we did not know why. Now when we reread them or perhaps when we share them with our children, these stories become alive with new and significant meanings. They may move us deeply, reflecting the changes that have occurred in our lives. This is one of the surest signs that we have become much wiser than we were. *Alice in Wonderland* is no longer a tale of a girl who falls asleep and follows a silly rabbit into a hole to enter into a dream world. It speaks to our hearts about what could happen to us if we allow our passive nature to take over. We are then able to pass through the veil that separates the known reality of everyday life from the other "inner reality" that also exists. Beyond this veil lies the land of the inner self, the place where all things are possible. All our hidden fears and desires are revealed at this level. Alice's experiences were a reflection of the contents of her own subconscious levels of mind. Some of these were positive experiences, while others were negative. But none were neutral. This is a very important point. Subconscious information is significant because we are emotionally tied to it. It doesn't matter if the emotions are positive or negative, desirable or undesirable. They must exist for any event to have life energy in the subconscious mind.

Finally, symbolic language allows stories to be passed on with minimal distortion. Symbols are usually very concrete. They are not dynamic as are abstract thoughts or philosophies. Their meanings change little with time. Thus, the Biblical parables of the talents, the sower, and the prodigal son convey the same messages that they have for the past two thousand years.

Personal Symbols

There are two types of symbols that are significant in dream analysis: personal and universal. Personal symbols are applicable only to us as individuals. They represent the people with whom we have strong or significant relationships. Personal symbols in a dream denote either our relationship with the symbol or the emotion the symbol evokes in us. Suppose we have a dream that includes our father. Obviously, his relationship to us is "father." The emotions that our father creates in us are based on how we interact with each other. We may feel that our strongest emotions toward him are "fear" or "resentment."

When a personal symbol appears in a dream, we need to record three things. First, we write down the person's name. Second, we note our relationship to him or her. This could be father, mother, sister, former boss, lover, enemy, friend, wife, childhood friend, and so on. Third, we put down the strongest feeling or reaction we have toward this person. This might be love, hate, trust, nervousness, respect, or fear, for example. Eventually, our personal symbols list includes everyone who has some importance to us. Below is an example of a personal symbols list.

Personal Symbols

PERSON'S NAME	RELATIONSHIP	EMOTIONAL REACTION
John Brady	father	resentment
Allen Brady	older brother	anger
Bradley Hopkins	friend	happiness
Kathy Jones	sister	irritation
Ellen Brady	mother	love
Joe Thomas	uncle	jealousy
Karen Brady	wife	love
Henry Stone	fellow worker	friendship
Rev Phillips	minister	respect
Hal Thomas	boss	fear

Universal Symbols

The second type of symbol is the universal symbol. This is not to be mistaken for the elusive archetypal symbol that is fixed within the deep recesses of the mind. Although there have been repeated attempts to verify archetypes, most attempts have obtained limited results. Jung did a lot of research on them, trying to extract the deeper meanings of symbols that had changed little over time. He believed that these meanings were created by the combined mind of humanity. Over countless ages, base definitions for each symbol were accumulated to form a "collective unconscious." Along with Jung, others have tried to derive the unique archetypal or base meaning of each symbol. Unfortunately, their methods obtained varying definitions that appeared to be biased by the conscious beliefs of the individuals tested. Attempts to create a dictionary of archetypal definitions have, for the most part, been unsuccessful. The mind has many levels of definitions for each symbol. Depending on an individual's beliefs, mood, intellect, and interests, the definitions will vary. Even the free association technique used by Jung was unable to remove individual bias. It was clear that a new method had to be found.

The dictionary of universal symbols at the back of this book was developed by using the synergic, or combined, mental energy of several psychics. Together, we tapped into the universal intelligence. The methodology was very simple. I used several people who were known psychics and were agreeable in helping me with this experiment. I went into a light meditative state. I pictured our energies joining each other on the inner planes or the deeper levels of mind. When this was accomplished, I asked for the definition of each symbol. The result was the dictionary.

Since the purpose of this book is to help individuals obtain practical and spiritual guidance, the definitions were gathered with this purpose in mind. Although these definitions are not the sought-after archetypal meanings, they will suffice until each of us is also able to tap into the universal intelligence and get guidance directly.

Most of the symbols given represent a whole catagory. In other words, any snake seen in a dream will represent all snakes. It does not matter that it is a cobra, python, garter, or milk snake. Similarly, any fish (guppy, shark, tuna, or bass) represents the universal symbol "fish." In some cases, such as in the animal kingdom, different species are listed because of the strong characteristics that they represent. Bear, fox, tiger, sheep, monkey, cat, horse, rat, and rabbit are among the individual animals listed.

5
Analyzing
Our Dreams

Having recorded a dream, we can start to analyze it. First, we identify what type of dream it is. There are two procedures that will help us accurately categorize our dreams.

The first and simplest method is to use the natural psychic ability that we all possess. If we ask our inner intelligence what type of dream we have had, we will receive an answer. This becomes easier as we gain confidence in our own psychic ability. (One of many known methods of developing and utilizing this ability is covered in detail in chapter 7.) Of course, there are some arguments against using this method. First, many people do not believe in their own psyche. Their reasoning is that it goes against their religious beliefs or scientific training. The problem is not one of principles, but of semantics. Christians call this level of mind prophetic. Science calls it intuition or inspiration. Calling our abilities psychic, prophetic, or intuitive doesn't change what they are. I tell my students if the process works, use it. Second, some people do not find this method reliable, but this is only because they lack self-confidence. However, this is a valid reason for choosing not to use the psyche. For these people, a second method is provided.

Identifying Psychic Dreams

Because psychic dreams are the easiest of the three types of dreams to identify, we discuss them before the others. First, they must be reasonable, i.e., they must comply with the laws of nature. They cannot include people flying on their own powers or walking through walls. But a psychic dream may be about another time and space. Therefore, we may see people wearing different kinds of clothes or living in some ancient or future society. Being reasonable is still the best test of a psychic dream.

There are two additional tests that should also be made. Although these tests are not conclusive by themselves, successfully meeting their criteria increases the probability that our dream was psychic. For the second test, we ask ourselves if the dream was very vivid, having a feeling of reality to the extent that differentiating it from an actual event is difficult. Psychic dreams have unusual depth and aliveness. The colors we experience shimmer and glow. The vividness of a dream tends to indicate that it was psychic.

Third, all psychic dreams evoke great emotions. A strong emotion, such as fear, anger, pain, joy, or excitement, formed our bond to the event in the dream. Thus, feeling a powerful emotion during the dream also indicates a psychic dream. When these three conditions are met (reasonable, vivid, and emotional), the dream is undoubtedly a psychic one.

The message of a psychic dream is simple. It is trying to prepare us for the future, even if we dream of the past. Whenever an upcoming event is causing us some concern, a dream will be created to indicate the probable outcome. Concern for someone in the family may cause a dream of the future. This happened to my mother long before I got into dream analysis. In her dream, my sister returned home to Hawaii after living in San Francisco for several years. My mother went into great detail on how real the dream was, how she could see every detail of my sister's return. A few days later, my sister actually paid us a surprise visit. She had not told anyone in the family that she was coming. Everyone was surprised. Everyone, that is, except my mother. She said that she already knew. She mentioned that my sister even wore the same outfit that she had seen in her dream.

Other events, such as an upcoming trip to South America, may be the stimulus for a dream of what life is like there or what you will see on your trip. An expectant couple may individually have dreams in which they have a glimpse of their child at some future date. Many years later, they may reexperience the content of their dream and say, "I've seen this before."

Psychic dreams are not limited to future events. Because dreams move through time, they are also able to retreat into the past. The South America trip may trigger a dream of the ancient Incas or life in the Amazon jungle. A planned European vacation may result in dreams of Rome under Julius Caesar or the days of knighthood. There is no real difference between a psychic view of the future or the past. Both are the result of your inner intelligence preparing you for something. This type of dream should be noted as a lesson in life.

Dreaming of a future event is no guarantee the event will take place. Free will gives each of us the ability to change every event previewed by a dream. Most of us will choose not to change our lives. Therefore, the future events probably will happen exactly as seen. No further analysis is required for a psychic dream.

Identifying Physical/Emotional Clearance Dreams

If a dream does not appear to be a psychic one, it is either a physical/emotional clearance dream or a spiritual guidance one. No clear division separates these two types of dreams. If a dream depicts some event that has been bothering us during the past few days, it is probably a clearance dream. Emotional or stress-producing situations, such as studying for an exam, arguing with our spouse, or feeling frustration with our co-workers, would fall into this category. Further analysis of clearance dreams is not necessary. The analysis method given in this chapter for spiritual guidance dreams can be applied, but only if we are curious. The primary purpose of a clearance dream is to release the emotional charge that some event has generated.

If the clearance dream is a repeating one, it then requires

more attention. It is beneficial for us to examine the problem and ask why it has continued to be a problem for such a long time. We often think an identified problem is insignificant. But the dream we remember when waking is usually the last dream of the night. This means that we have spent most of the night trying to clear the emotions that were created but have failed. So we wake up in the morning remembering our clearance dream and feeling very tired.

It is possible to release the emotional charge of events *before* going to sleep. We can do this with a simple mental exercise. First, we need to sit or lie in a comfortable position. Then we begin to review our day. Whenever we recall any strong emotional event, we mentally forgive the other party for their actions. Finally, and most importantly, we must forgive ourselves. Our forgiveness must not be just an intellectual exercise. It must be expressed sincerely, with deep, heartfelt emotion. Only then will there be a meaningful inner release. When done properly, we will rest easier and will be able to allow our sleep state to work on the spiritual guidance dreams.

Identifying Spiritual Guidance Dreams

If a dream is not an obvious clearance one, it is probably a spiritual guidance dream. These are the dreams that should interest us the most. Contained in their symbols is the message we all require to guide us through life.

We begin by underlining the universal and personal symbols found in the text of our recorded dream. A colored pen will make the symbols stand out from the rest of the text. Above each symbol, write the definition as found in the personal symbols list and the dictionary of universal symbols. An example is shown below:

> *same as "sunrise": emotional   purification*
> ◉ I woke up in the underline{morning} and went to the underline{bathroom}.
> *image   healing*
> Looking into the underline{mirror}, I saw that I was underline{green}. I thought
> *release tension*
> that this was really funny and began to underline{laugh}. I thought

creation
that someone had played a joke on me and had <u>painted</u>
    healing   not real yet without personality
me <u>green</u> during the <u>night</u>. I <u>undressed</u> and got into the
regeneration cleansing   complete self
<u>bathtub</u> and <u>scrubbed</u> my <u>whole body</u>. But, there was no
                characteristic   regeneration
way that I could get this <u>color</u> off. I got out of the <u>bathtub</u>
                    image   healing
and got in front of the <u>mirror</u>, but I was still <u>green</u>. Even
mental energy   healing   *ordered life*
my <u>hair</u> was <u>green</u>, so I thought I would <u>comb</u> it.
        mental energy
When I tried to comb it, my <u>hair</u> all fell out and I was com-
    loss of energy
pletely <u>bald</u>. I thought, "This is stupid, it can't be hap-
        released tension   blame others
pening to me." I <u>laughed</u> and thought that the <u>person</u> who
    creation   *same as "bald"*
had <u>painted</u> me must have also <u>shaved my hair</u> off and
false energy   *personality*
put a <u>wig</u> on me. So I grabbed some <u>clothes</u>, and they also
        healing
turned <u>green</u> when I put them on. I thought, "Whatever it

is, there is no way that I can control it, so I may as well

just enjoy it."

Developing a Theme

If we read a dream focusing on the definitions written above
each symbol, we can develop its theme. A theme is a simple and
impersonal statement that summarizes the underlying message
of the dream. There is no one correct theme, but all themes will
generally point in the same direction. For example, the theme
of the novel *Gone with the Wind* might be "Love and hate are
driving forces" or "War is hell," depending on your focus. The
theme of the New Testament of the Bible might be "Someone

loves mankind" or "Great teachers always appear when needed."
Note that the name of Jesus is not written into these themes,
which keeps them impersonal. We do not want to limit the
message of a dream to a particular individual. This is especially
important since dreams are primarily about the dreamer and do
not involve other persons directly. For the example dream given
above, the theme might be expressed as, "A healing is taking
place." For complex dreams, there may be several themes. All
themes should be recorded in our notebook, somewhere in the
margin next to the dream text.

Analyzing a Dream

Once the theme (or themes) has been recorded, we can start to
develop an overall plot, a story of what is being said. We should
always keep the theme in mind to avoid straying from the real
intent of the dream. We begin by listing statements that the
dream is making. The following list is an example for the dream
related above.

1. Regeneration and healing began while I was visiting a
place for healing.
2. I could recognize that some changes were happening,
especially through the release of tension.
3. Changes are occurring in my whole body, even my personality is changing.
4. I am resisting the changes on an unconscious level.
5. I should accept this change because I will benefit
from it.

Next we try to tie the above elements into a more complete
analysis. We should keep in mind that there is no *one* correct
analysis for any given dream. My analysis of the above dream
was as follows:

The dreamer had gone to a healing center of some kind
for help with rebalancing his body. This healing center
could be either a doctor, healer, or church. After the visit,
changes are taking place but not in the way that the

dreamer expected. On an unconscious level, the dreamer is resisting the changes because the changes are not what he anticipated. Changes in the physical body are easily accepted, but the subtle changes make the dreamer uneasy. The changes in thinking, outlook, and personality are much more difficult to handle. Deep inside, the dreamer knows all the changes are for the best. Other benefits are also coming into his life. He has only to accept this process on a conscious level, and things will quickly fall into place.

Our analysis should be studied to see how well it fits into our real-life situation. The area the dream is describing should be apparent to us. If it is not, we should read the theme again and try to find other situations that may apply. But we shouldn't get discouraged if we are unable at first to understand the content of a dream. Our inner intelligence will repeat the message, although different or modified symbols may appear in subsequent dreams. The message will eventually get through, provided there is still the need for it. (In order to get familiar with this technique, a number of sample dreams with an analysis and a brief description of the dreamer's life situation are included in chapter 7.)

Once the message of the dream is understood, it is time to take action. Recognizing a problem is usually not enough. We are all too adept at putting off doing anything or at making some kind of an excuse. We need to uncover the real source of our problem and then correct it. Once we have, the possibilities are unlimited. *We are never given any task that is beyond our ability to accomplish.* The guidance of our dreams comes from our own deeper levels of consciousness. Our own inner intelligence exposes a problem and then proposes a solution. By following and acting upon the messages in our dreams, we can make great progress in our lives. Each day, we will advance steadily toward completing the mission we began when we chose to come into this world.

6

Common Dreams

S piritual guidance dreams can be categorized into thirteen general themes. Approximately ninety percent of all dreams will fall into one of the following categories: chasing or being chased, which includes searching, avoidance, and entrapment; flying; falling; birth and death; illness, disease, and restoration of health; injury and rejuvenation; fighting; driving a vehicle; being in water; sexual encounters; being detached and an observer; being in a school or classroom, teaching, or learning; and transcendental experiences.

Chase Dreams

The chase is the most commonly remembered dream. In it, we identify ourselves as either the chaser or the one being chased. If we are the chaser, whatever we are chasing is a goal in our life. It symbolizes what we are trying to become. As long as we continue the chase in our dreams, we are still working to achieve this goal. When we finally have a dream in which we catch what we were chasing, we have either obtained or are about to obtain our goal. The following illustrate this form of chase dream with symbolic goals:

Dreamer chases a dog. Dreamer is attempting to become more dependable, a better parent or guardian to his family.
Dreamer chases a cat. Dreamer is probably working on improving a relationship or a marriage.
Dreamer chases someone with a lot of money. Dreamer is trying to gain wealth but is unable to find it.
Dreamer chases something illusive, an invisible thing. Dreamer is spending a lot of time trying to achieve true fulfillment in his life. He is aware of the emptiness of his life but is unable to fill this need because he is unable to see what his actual goals are.
Dreamer chases someone with a sail. Dreamer is looking for the creative spirit that is within himself.
Dreamer chases someone who is carrying a bucket of water and finally catches him. Dreamer needs an emotional cleansing and is about to receive it.

If the chase dream is a repeating one, we are somehow frustrated in attaining our goal. Philosophically, we sometimes lose sight of our goal in life. We become so intent on the chase that the goal is no longer important. The chase is no longer a means to an end but has become an end in itself. We are like the dieter who continues to go from one diet to another. The dieter constantly talks about his diets, explaining the latest and how it compares to all the other diets that he has tried. He lives to diet and to lose weight. The fact that his weight losses are never permanent points out that this compulsive dieting has become an end in itself. So it is with the repeating chase dream, indicating our pursuit of an elusive goal we never really intend to catch.

The other side of the chase dream is one in which we are being chased. Again, we must identify what is chasing us. It represents what we are already in the process of becoming. It is just a matter of time before we assume the symbol's attributes. (Refer to the dictionary of universal symbols or your personal symbols list to obtain the characteristics of the thing or person doing the chasing.) Examples of this kind of dream are interpreted as follows:

Dreamer is chased by a dog. Dreamer is becoming more dependable, a better parent or guardian to his family.

Dreamer is chased by a fish. Dreamer is becoming more spiritual and religious.

Dreamer is chased by a tiger. Dreamer is becoming more cruel and wrathful.

Dreamer is chased by someone he knows. Dreamer's personality is becoming more and more like that of the person chasing him.

Rock rolls down hill to crush dreamer. Dreamer is becoming more stable, in better harmony with his environment.

Dreamer is chased by an elusive, invisible person or thing. Dreamer is being pushed by his own inner drive to get on a more spiritual path.

Dreamer is chased by a demon. Dreamer is using his energy for his own personal gain (selfish). The reward may be achieved, but the penalty that will be incurred has not been considered.

Dreamer is chased by a mummy. Dreamer is working to preserve his outer appearance. He is working on either his body through diet and exercise or his appearance through cosmetic changes.

Finally there is the type of chase dream in which we are neither the chaser nor the one being chased. Instead, we are an interested observer, usually watching the scene from an elevated position. It would appear that we could be identified as either the chaser or the one being chased. Usually, however, we are the one being chased. We are becoming whatever is chasing us. These dreams are analyzed in much the same manner as the other dreams in which we are being chased. There is one important difference. We do not see ourselves as being responsible for the changes that are taking place. Therefore, we witness the chase from a safe distance, separating ourselves from the drama that is occuring. The following examples illustrate this:

Dreamer observes a fish being chased by a snake. Dreamer's religious beliefs are being changed into inner spiritual development and awareness.

Dreamer observes a monkey being chased by fire.
Dreamer has become totally unconscious of inner drives.
Situations in his life will quickly make him aware what
these drives and desires are.
Dreamer observes an old man being chased by the wind.
Energy is returning to the dreamer. He will probably credit
a healer or a place of healing for the change.

Once we recognize what is happening, we are able to take
charge of our lives. If we do not like what is happening, we can
do something else. Is that all there is to it? Not usually. We always have reasons, justifications, and considerations why it is
impossible for us to make changes. But these are the decisions
of life. They are the spice that gives each of our lives a unique
flavor.

The Search Dream

The search is another form of the chase. The analysis is identi-
cal to our chasing something or someone. But the search dream
is driven by our own awareness that something is missing in
our lives. We may not be aware what is missing, but we sense
that it is very important to us. The driving force is our need
to do something, even if we have no idea what it is. The action
in a search dream is methodical and slow compared to a chase
dream. We are always moving closer to our goal. In time, our
goal may even change or evolve to a higher goal. But we continue our deliberate efforts, ever hopeful of finding the missing
link in our lives.

The Avoidance Dream

An avoidance dream is similar to a chase dream in which we are
being chased. In the dream, we somehow intuitively know that
something is after us. We may not consciously recognize who
or what is coming to get us, but we know it is coming. So our
dream is keyed toward avoiding the oncoming situation. Analyzing an avoidance dream is the same as analyzing a dream of

being chased, except that in an avoidance dream, our effort to avoid change is not as strong as in a chase dream.

> *Dreamer is avoiding a dog.* Dreamer does not want to accept family responsibilities.
> *Dreamer is avoiding a fish.* Dreamer is denying any interest in becoming more spiritual and religious.
> *Dreamer is avoiding someone he knows.* Dreamer is not accepting that his personality is becoming more and more like that of the person he is avoiding.

The Entrapment Dream

This is the final step in the chase dream sequence. In a chase dream, we run out of fear, perhaps without any idea what is chasing us. In an avoidance dream, we are inwardly aware of being chased and choose not to face our pursuer. Finally, after exhausting all possibilities to avoid the outcome, we realize we have to face the natural results of our actions. This is when we have a dream of being trapped. We have boxed ourselves into a corner where there is no way out. To obtain the message of the dream, we need to identify the symbolic meaning of what or who has trapped us. The following will illustrate this:

> *Dreamer is trapped by a dragon.* Dreamer is finally ready to get healed.
> *Dreamer is trapped by a professor of philosophy.* Dreamer is about to learn a lot more about life, gaining an understanding of many fields.
> *Dreamer is trapped by walls.* Dreamer has created limitations on his life that prevent him from having new experiences.
> *Dreamer is trapped by mountains all around him.* Dreamer feels that his life is limited by his idealistic goals. His life has been directed toward accomplishing these goals, but he feels he is unable to complete them. But these goals are about to be realized.

Flying Dreams

All dreams of flying indicate high aspirations of one sort or another. We first identify who or what is flying. If it is ourselves as we normally are, then we are spending a lot of time trying to obtain some idealistic goal. If we are symbolically disguised, then whatever the symbol represents is the aspect of our personality that has high aspirations. For example, if we look like a teacher out of our past, then we have high expectations of and aspirations for our teaching ability. If we are dressed as a doctor, then we want to improve our healing abilities. We also need to note how high we fly in a dream. If we fly very high but also swoop down to touch the ground, we are able to bring our ideals "down to earth," where we may apply them to our lives. If we spend most of our time flying in the clouds or in a fog, we are probably out of touch with reality. We are unable to see things clearly and may find it difficult to function in the world around us. Flying very high often indicates that our aspirations are so high that they are not practical and may be difficult to apply.

Dreams of Falling or Floating Away

The sensation of floating away when falling asleep is a universal phenomenon. Almost everyone has experienced this at one time or another. Although the sensation is familiar to most of us, the explanation of what is happening is not. When we fall asleep, our consciousness leaves our body. This consciousness is known by many names. Some of us call it our spirit or soul. Others refer to it as the astral body or point of awareness. When this transference takes place, and it does every night, it gives us that feeling of rising or floating away. This process, strange as it may seem, is not entirely unfamiliar. It is reflected in our language. We commonly say, "I fell asleep," or "I was gone," or "I just drifted off." Fell where? Gone or drifted where? Even when we talk about daydreaming, we often hear the expression, "I was off somewhere." These statements hint that our consciousness does, in fact, leave our physical body when we fall asleep.

At the end of the night, our consciousness once again returns to rejoin our physical body. As it gets close, it becomes rigid and positions itself directly above our physical body. Slowly it floats down until it realigns itself with the body. This results in the sensation of falling that so many of us have just before waking. The fall feels very long, and we never quite hit the ground. Instead we are suddenly awake. When asked about this sensation, we usually conclude that it was just another part of our dream and dismiss it as another natural, but unexplainable, phenomenon.

Two unusual things may happen as the merging takes place. The first occurs when we are really tired and in a deep sleep. If anything happens to startle us and we are jolted awake, we may find it difficult to do anything. The jarring has caused our consciousness to instantly return to our physical body. Once in a while, our consciousness and physical body do not align themselves properly. We have difficulty thinking clearly or even moving with any degree of coordination. This condition passes quickly, but we have a strange feeling while it lasts.

The other condition occurs when our consciousness returns and in the rejoining is very much out of alignment. We may find ourselves unable to move any part of our body. Many have described this phenomena as the feeling of being tied down or restrained by some strange and unseen force. No matter how hard we struggle, it is impossible to move. Once in a while, we may be able to open our eyes and see, but the rest of our body still feels pinned down. Fear comes, and we may even try to scream, but nothing happens. Eventually we become exhausted and finally fall asleep again. When we awaken, everything is back to normal. These experiences are usually dismissed as part of a dream. A few people have mentioned their concern that some dark force was trying to take them over or even trying to kill them. There is nothing to worry about. An occasional misalignment is natural and happens to everyone. The best thing for us to do is to simply relax and fall asleep again. Everything will be back to normal by morning.

Dreams of Birth or Death

At first glance, it may appear strange to combine both birth and death into a single category. Although they seem completely different, they are a part of a single process. Of course, they are at the opposite poles of the process. Neither birth nor death can exist without the other. It is easy to see that there cannot be a death without a birth first. It is a little more difficult to see that there cannot be a birth until there is a death or an ending. The ancient Hindus stated this in the following way. They said that a person is unable to fill his treasure chest with jewels while it is still full of rocks. The first thing he has to do is empty out all the rocks. Life is a similar process of change. Good things, opportunities, and fortunes are constantly passing by. Some people always seem able to make full use of these. Most of us, however, never seem to be able to touch any of the more desirable things in life. We hold on to our "rocks," the old things and ideas that we have. As long as we cling to the old, there is no space for our "jewels," for anything new and better to come into our lives. Therefore, death or an ending allows birth or a beginning. Birth guarantees eventual death. Death guarantees the birth of the new.

Spiritual guidance dreams of death and birth give us the same message. A death in a dream is an indication that something is about to end. Whatever is dying can be interpreted as that aspect of ourselves that is being changed. If the death is not of us as we recognize ourselves, we need to look up in the dictionary the characteristics of the symbol representing us. The following show how dreams of death are interpreted:

> *Dreamer fights with a tiger and the tiger dies.* The dreamer's cruel and wrathful nature is under his control and is ending.
> *Dreamer sees an owl that dies.* Dreamer's passive nature is ending without any apparent effort on his own.
> *Dreamer catches a blue fish that dies.* Dreamer's belief about life (especially as taught in traditional religion) is ending.
> *Dreamer sees a bird shot down by a hunter.* Dreamer's

high ideals are impractical at this time. The requirements of life have made him face reality.

A doll the dreamer had is destroyed. Dreamer will no longer blame others for his shortcomings and difficulties.

A dam that the dreamer owned breaks. Some obstacle that has been stopping the flow of energy in the dreamer's life has been removed.

In a similar manner, any dream of birth or creation will indicate a new aspect that is being added to our lives. What is being created can be identified by consulting the dictionary of universal symbols. The following examples show how dreams of birth are interpreted:

A baby is born that looks like the dreamer's father. The dreamer is taking on some of the characteristics of his father. This would be the strongest characteristic as noted in our personal symbols list (see chapter 4).

An egg with clothes inside is given to the dreamer. The dreamer is changing his behavior or personality.

A new set of teeth comes in and replaces the old set. The dreamer will be better able to communicate with others or be able to communicate in a different manner, such as through art or music.

Dreamer's wife gives birth to a new baby. Dreamer will be changing his personality and his behavior. This change will not only be directed toward his relationship with his wife but also toward his relationships with his family and others.

Dreams of Illness, Disease, or Restoration of Health

The cause of disease is found in the word itself, "dis-ease." Put another way, diseases result from a lack of ease or our inability to relax. Tension is the deadly by-product of an industrial society. Our inability to adapt quickly enough to the rapid growth and change in our technological and industrial world creates this tension. The cure? Rest and relaxation. Simple enough, but there never seems to be any time for rest. If it's not work, then it's the kids, or the family, or any one of a thousand things that needs to be done. Even vacations, during which we are supposed to have a chance to "vacate" or "empty" ourselves, often turn into a mad rush as we hurry from one place to the next. We have to return to work to "rest" from our vacations. Our bodies and minds adjust to this constantly rising level of tension, but eventually there will be a point when this is no longer possible. When the body can no longer keep up this pace, it breaks down. An illness is created. Finally we have a valid reason to stop ourselves completely and allow ourselves to rest. Feeling miserable will force us to remain in bed for a few days. The illness will last for as long as it takes our body to recuperate. Rest will remove tension, allow recovery, and restore health. Dreams of getting ill are a signal that the body and mind are in need of rest. If we resist these signals, illness may result. The following are dreams of illnesses that have been interpreted with the use of the dictionary.

> *Dreamer has a headache.* Dreamer is mentally tired and in need of rest.
> *Dreamer has a lung problem with a bad cough.* Dreamer is making the wrong use of his energy and should conserve it.
> *Dreamer has a high fever.* Dreamer is using his body's own energy to heal himself. Rest is recommended to support this action.

A dream of a serious disease indicates that a more acute condition is present. It is imperative to stop the condition being implied by the disease. The type of disease will identify what is causing our tension. Additionally, we need to note where the disease is. Skin cancer does not have the same interpretation as bone cancer, even though both are cancers. The following illustrate how diseases in dreams are interpreted:

> *Dreamer has an ulcer and his stomach hurts.* Stomach is the healing center, and dreamer is fighting his own inner healing process. His resistance is shown by the pain.
> *Dreamer has a cancer in his foot.* Dreamer is worried about things that support him. He is trying to reinforce the support but in the wrong manner.

Dreamer has warts and growths on his skin. Dreamer's protective, psychological barrier is being penetrated by those around him. He must somehow stop being emotionally affected by others.

Dreamer has an enlarged heart and surgeons will operate. Dreamer has a lot of love and needs to share it with others.

There are other dreams in which a healing is in progress. This may be interpreted as a correction of an imbalance in our lives. The disease or illness we have in the dream will point out the area that is being healed, such as:

Dreamer was going bald but his hair is beginning to grow back. Dreamer is receiving more energy, especially to do mental work.

Dreamer's skin was dry and flaking off but is now getting better. Dreamer's protection from negativity was very weak and is now being corrected.

Dreams of Injury and Rejuvenation

Life is change. Everything is constantly ending as one thing and becoming another. Birth and death, as described earlier, are forms of change. Beside these major changes, many smaller changes are taking place in all aspects of our lives. Why is the process of change so difficult? Why is the loss that precedes change so painful? Part of the answer is the inner fear that is created when someone or something that provided support is removed. Life is scary enough without having these lifelines cut. But loss is the natural consequence of change. In addition to the fear of loss, our egos also come into play. Not having something or losing someone hurts our pride. In an effort to protect ourselves, we want to hold onto the old. Once we understand that losses are a part of the process, perhaps we will find change easier to accept.

As with birth and death dreams, dreams of injury indicate that an old condition must be removed or eliminated before a new condition can come into being. The severity of the injury will indicate how complete and permanent the change will be.

A minor injury, such as a sprain or broken bone, means the change will be short-lived. A more serious injury, such as a surgical removal or an amputation, indicates a more permanent change. (The attributes of the injuries or removed body components are in the dictionary under "body.") These dreams can be interpreted in the following manner.

> *Dreamer's hair falls off.* Dreamer is losing mental energy or the ability to mentally process information.
> *Dreamer has his arms cut off.* Dreamer's ability to make dramatic changes in his life is inhibited.
> *Dreamer has foot amputated to save his life.* Dreamer is in the process of changing his belief system.

In the examples above, none of the injuries were self-inflicted. We would interpret this to mean that we feel that the real cause of change is from outside ourselves. So if things are going wrong in our lives, we want to blame someone or something else. Only if things begin to go right will we take credit. This response, however, is only our outer thinking. Inwardly, we will still feel that someone or something else really deserves the credit. If, however, we have a dream in which we inflict the injury on ourself, we are aware that we are the only one who is responsible for everything that happens in our life.

Finally, our dream may include a segment in which we are healed of our injury or an amputated organ or limb rejuvenates. This kind of dream says our problem is being resolved and a new or different aspect is becoming real. The rejuvenated body part will begin to feel like new, much better than the old. If it does not, a reversion has taken place. The body part will look and feel like the old component that was lost. This indicates that we have not made much progress and have reverted to our old ways. The following examples will illustrate this:

> *Dreamer regrows his lost arms.* Dreamer is gaining new ability in helping him make further changes in his life. Making changes will be easier in the future.
> *Dreamer's amputated foot grows back but still feels like the tired old foot that was lost.* Dreamer had a chance to release his old beliefs and take on new ones that were more adaptable to his present situations and lifestyle. Unfortunately, he has reverted back to the old beliefs.

Fighting Dreams

Fighting is another of the very common themes. The message of all dreams of physical conflict is that we need to resolve an inner conflict. Inner turmoil is created whenever we have difficulty deciding between several choices. Interpretations of fighting dreams are shown in the following examples:

> *Dreamer fights with a cat.* Dreamer has an inner conflict about a relationship, probably his marriage.
> *Dreamer fights with family members.* Dreamer has a conflict about his responsibilities to his family.
> *Dreamer fights with a knight in armor.* Dreamer has an inner conflict about what is right and wrong.

If our dream is not of ourself fighting but of someone or something else having a fight, the interpretation of the dream changes slightly. It means that we are not ready to accept responsibility for our part in some conflict. Dreams of this type are interpreted as follows:

> *A cat fights with dreamer's husband.* Dreamer views problems in her relationship with her husband as being his problem or his fault.
> *An old man fights with several young knights.* Dreamer is about to release many old ideas about life and his value system. He is resisting the release and feels that the problem is not really one that he needs to work on.
> *A crocodile fights with the dreamer's father.* The dreamer is subconsciously blaming his father for his problems.

Dreams of Driving a Vehicle

Any dream in which we are driving a vehicle shows a period in our life when things are going well. The type of vehicle does not matter. A jet plane and a horse and carriage have the same basic meaning. The speed of the vehicle, however, shows our potential for action. The faster the vehicle is capable of going, the greater our potential. Obviously, we have much more capability if we were riding in an airplane instead of on a bicycle. But if the dream shows us creeping along in a jet at one mile an hour, we are certainly not making use of our potential. We are really capable of much more. In the same way, if our dream depicts us riding very fast on a bicycle, we are probably making full use of whatever we have to work with.

In another form of this type of dream, we are riding on the back of another person. (This person should be on our personal symbols list.) Whatever the person represents symbolically is the aspect of our personality that is carrying us through life. If we are carried by a strong authority figure, we are making progress by also being strongly authoritarian. Conversely, if the person carrying us represents a loving figure, we are making progress by being loving toward others. It is also important to note whether the symbolic person carrying us is doing so willingly or with reluctance. If willingly, the aspect is deeply ingrained, controlled, and we may not want to alter it. We really don't see anything wrong with what we are doing or the way we are and will not make any efforts to change. On the other hand, if our carrier is reluctant, we realize our actions are no longer appropriate. It becomes a simple matter for us to change.

There are also dreams in which we are riding an animal. Other than riding horses, these are quite rare. The willingness of the animal to carry us is also important here. If the animal is willing, we are satisfied with having this animal's characteristics as part of our personality. We are willing to live with these attributes in order to make progress. On the other hand, if the animal is unwilling, we seek domination over the characteristic. We are having a hard time justifying our actions to ourself. Dreams of riding an animal are interpreted as follows:

> *Dreamer rides a horse at a gallop.* Dreamer is moving through life with much determination and making much progress.
> *Dreamer struggles to ride a tiger and makes very little real movement.* Dreamer is trying to keep his vengeful and cruel nature in check. He is making only limited progress and is struggling with his life.
> *Dreamer rides a pet monkey.* Dreamer is in control of his unconscious desires.
> *Dreamer has some difficulty riding a lamb.* Dreamer feels that he is being noble by sacrificing himself.

Dreamer struggles to make a donkey move. Dreamer is struggling with his own stubbornness and is not making any real progress.

Dreams of Being in Water

All experiences in our lives become a part of our memories. Memories that have a strong emotion attached to them can later cause an emotional problem. An event that occurs without any significant emotion simply enters into our memories as another cataloged fact. When that fact, such as a friend's phone number, is recalled, there is no feeling attached. There is no reactionary behavior that can come from it. But when an emotional event occurs, every emotion experienced is registered. When this event comes to mind at some later date, the same emotions are felt once again. When these emotions are very strong, this memory may develop into an emotional hang-up.

When one of our emotional memories is triggered by a chance meeting with someone or something, the event and all the attached emotions are recalled. If the emotions were good, we will have a positive bias toward whatever is happening. We already feel good and believe that everything will be fine. But if the emotions were negative, the bias will be negative. We already dislike the other person, place, or situation. What is happening is making us uncomfortable, and we want to leave or attack.

Once we recognize our response, we can make the necessary corrections for our bias. We will know that our feelings are a product of the past and have nothing to do with the present. But most people are unable to do this. Because this process occurs within the subconscious mind, they cannot realize what is happening. They are unable to compensate for their reactions to a given situation.

There is nothing wrong with our emotional memory mechanism. It is absolutely perfect for what it does. It is a survival mechanism. We all know that fire can hurt us. Somewhere in the past, we all learned this, either from the pain of being burned or the punishment we received for playing with fire.

This emotional memory was entered into the subconscious levels of our mind. Later, we had the opportunity to experience fire again. As we got close to it, our subconscious mind automatically recalled the emotional memory, and we reacted negatively to the fire. This demonstrates the preservation instinct of the subconscious mind.

In the realm of human relationships, this type of reaction is inappropriate. For example, we may have had a bad experience with someone named John. When we meet a person who somehow resembles John, our subconscious mind will trigger the negative emotions associated with our previous experience. Usually, the memory is not recalled at all, and only the feelings are restimulated. So we are ready to react to anything the new person might do based on our bias against John. The new person already has a couple of strikes against him. If he does anything that even reminds us of John, he is rejected. In order to change our automatic reactions based on emotional memories, the emotional tie to the events must be erased. This process is called an emotional cleansing.

Water symbolizes our emotional level of consciousness. Whenever we see it in a dream, it touches our emotions. Whenever we or anyone else in our dream gets wet, we are undergoing an emotional cleansing of some sort. It does not matter how we get wet. Our dream may show us getting wet with ocean spray while walking along the beach, taking a shower, or walking under a building's fire sprinklers. The message is always the same, indicating the release of an emotional memory.

The degree of cleansing is depicted by the amount of washing we receive. If the cleansing is deep and complete, much more than a simple, superficial one, the release is also very deep and complete. The emotional glue that has been keeping past problems "stuck" is being scrubbed away. Taking a good bath with soap and water or being run through a washing machine are forms of deeper cleansing. If the washing makes the water dirty, then a lot of negativity has been released. On the other hand, if the washing is done with dirty water, the problem is being only superficially removed. The cleansing is not a good one and only appears to be a real cleansing. The degree of cleansing is also symbolized by the depth of water. If a dream finds us diving deep to the bottom of the ocean, then the cleansing is very complete. The problem the dream worked on may have been a repeating situation. The depth indicates how deep the dream went to reach the root cause of the problem and remove it. Dreams of cleansing with water are interpreted in the following examples:

Dreamer washes his hands and feet only. Dreamer is preparing to make changes in his life.
Dreamer takes a shower, and his clothes melt off. The dreamer has removed a lot of negativity. The changes that he experiences will be mostly in his personality.
Dreamer has clothes washed and puts clean clothes on without taking a bath. Dreamer appears to be trying to improve himself and how others see him. Deep within he remains the same.
Dreamer cleans and washes out his garage with soap and water. Dreamer is confronting his inhibitions, probably sexual, and is taking steps to correct them.

Dreams of Sexual Encounters

Sexual encounters are possibly the most interesting to experience and the most fascinating to interpret. Sex and sexual fantasies comprise a large part of our lives. There are many different levels from which we can interpret sexual dreams. On one level, a sex dream may be a way of fulfilling a desire. We may be in love with someone in particular or the ideal person of our dreams. In either case, the dream serves as a relief valve, a way of venting the tension created by our fantasy. Once the pressure has been relieved, we are able to get some rest and eventually fall asleep. The dream provides us a physical/emotional clearance. The sexual tension that has been building is identified and finally released by the dream. These dreams usually occur very early in the dream cycle and are not usually remembered when waking in the morning.

On a deeper level, dreams of sex will make us aware of hidden sexual desires or fears. These are usually buried so deep within our subconscious minds that we are not really aware of them. Under the right conditions, a memory might be triggered that causes some very strong feelings to surface. A chance encounter may result in an immediate, strong sexual desire for someone. Unaware of the triggering mechanism, we can be fooled into thinking the feeling is real. We have no way of knowing that the memory is completely biasing the encounter and coloring the experience. Our sexual dream will attempt to shed some light on the incident and act as a relief valve. It will reenact the past, showing why the strong emotions are there. In doing so, it will release much of the emotional tension that exists.

On a still deeper level, dreams of sex reveal our need for love. Love is such a necessary part of our lives that we spend a lot of time looking for it. It is the main theme of our movies, our music, our poetry, and even our dreams. Unfortunately, love is not a commodity that is easily identified. It is an elusive state that is impossible to define. So we settle for something with more measurable substance. We begin to equate sex with love. Sex is convenient. It is easily identified, measured, and evaluated. Even in our language we substitute the word "love" for "sex." We use common phrases such as "Let's make love" or "He's a good lover."

Digressing a moment here, it is important to understand what love is. We can best understand love by realizing what it is not. It is not something that we can get from someone else. It is not something we can steal or buy. Nor can we be made to give love because we are legally bound to, as in marriage. We cannot store love, to be used when required at some future date. Love exists only under the purest of conditions. It is the ultimate in unlimited sharing, the pure exchange of etheric energies. Therefore, at this deeper level, our sexual dreams are identifying a real lack in our lives and providing us some relief.

Having a dream of sexual intercourse may also be showing us how we are trying to bring together different aspects of our lives. This concept of spiritual unity may be a little difficult to grasp. Within each of us, there is a basic desire to achieve a unification within ourselves. We desire a life in which we are not torn between being either male or female. Physically, we are one or the other. Emotionally, we are neither, but a combina-

tion of both. Usually, one of the two dominates. Yet the similarities between the sexes are greater than the differences. This
concept of unification or oneness within is difficult to understand, but it becomes easier as we mature spiritually.

Differentiating these levels of sexual dreams can be resolved
by our self-awareness. Our attitudes and situations indicate the
source of our sexual dreams. If we are mainly involved in having
physical relationships and sexual encounters, our sex dreams
are simply releasing any tension from sexual frustration. If our
present lifestyle denies sex for any reason, our sex dreams are
also a means of releasing the buildup of physical tension. If we
are experiencing a powerful relationship, with either strong attraction or repulsion to our partner, our sexual dreams are trying to reveal the situations that have created these strong feelings and are working to release them. Finally, for those who are
deeply involved in some form of inner search for their answers
about life, sexual dreams reveal the need for real love or a more
unitive life. These latter are the sexual dreams of the highest
level.

Dreams of Detachment and Observation

These are also common dreams. Normally, we are active par-
ticipants in our dreams. On occasion, we may find ourselves
being drawn away from the action. This withdrawing is often
accompanied by a feeling of floating. We find ourselves either
overlooking the scene or watching the action from a safe distance, as if we were watching a program on television. We feel
that we are not a part of what is happening. This detachment
may continue throughout the dream. At other times, we may
find our point of awareness returning and once again we partic-
ipate in the action.

In all cases, the message is the same. When we become detached from the action in the dream, we feel we are not responsible for what the dream is saying. Consciously, we may believe
that someone or something else is responsible for the situation
we find ourselves in. The purpose of the dream is to inform us
we are avoiding responsibility. Once we acknowledge this, we
can take care of our problem.

Dreams of a School or Classroom Scene, Teaching, or Learning

These dreams are not very common. They are triggered by situations that bring up an emotional memory. Somehow, we must overcome our feelings from this memory and deal with the present situation. For example, at a party we meet someone who makes us uncomfortable, although we are not sure why. We would rather not have anything to do with him, but because of a mutual friend, we are almost obligated to be sociable. In the course of the evening, we find this person to be quite nice. That night, we have a dream of being in a classroom. We are being confronted by different people. We try to run away, but we are trapped by others. Finally, we confront these people, and they run away. Thus, the lesson of the day is reinforced by the dream.

The lesson depicted is what we are learning. It does not matter whether we are a student or a teacher in the dream. Eastern philosophy says the best teachers are the ones who learn while teaching. We are only here to learn. How we learn is totally up to us.

On a few rare occasions, a lesson may not be about the actual subject matter being taught, but about the relationship between ourselves and the other members of the class. The following illustrates this type of dream:

> ◐ I remember being in a classroom. It was not a very large room and reminded me of a classroom that I had when I was very young. There were seven students in the class, six others besides myself. The room was actually the basement of the school building and was quite cold. The teacher was discussing the significance of women in the history of our country. The teacher was giving a whole list of facts, but she was not really paying attention to the class. The others in the class were laughing among themselves. They were all boys, and I was the only girl. I got very upset with their behavior. I told them to pay attention to the lecture, and that made them laugh even more. One of them yelled at me to leave if I didn't like it. I began

to yell at them, and they all began yelling back. The teacher finally got annoyed at all the noise and also yelled for all of us to pay attention to her. No one would listen, and the yelling continued. I woke up with a start.

Obviously, the teacher's lecture is not the real point of the dream. The person who had this dream, a woman, is having trouble relating to others. Discussions with her revealed she was having difficulty communicating with her coworkers. The dream not only revealed this but predicted the situation would not be ending in the near future. It further revealed she was part of the problem, even though she felt she was blameless. Her actual solution to the problem was to find herself another job.

The Transcendental Experience

These are rare experiences that almost always defy casual description. Transcendental dreams stagger our imagination and totally put us into another world, another level of existence. Some people say such a dream is like a hallucination. Some have described a transcendental dream as a world of lights or one beyond time and space, or a creative experience beyond anything imaginable. Perhaps we can get a better understanding by reading two such experiences.

● This dream was a very strange one. In it, I was taken by someone to another place. There were many things, like colors and different sensations that kept coming at me. My guide seemed to be enjoying how astonished I felt as I stood in awe. From somewhere, I don't know where, there was a voice that spoke very softly to me. It said that I was looking for the meaning of my life in the wrong ways. It said that there were many things that I had to do, and the task that I chose was very difficult. Help would be there, if I ever got on the right path. Then came a tremendous outpouring of love and understanding from the direction of the voice. It was more beautiful than anything I, or anyone else, could ever imagine. From that point, things seemed so different in my life. I've taken a good look at my life and have decided to work from a different point of view. Life will never be the same for me again.

◑ I dreamt that I was on the outside of a pyramid. The pyramid was totally white, with a golden top. At each corner was another smaller pyramid, but made of gold. There were several people who were giving me some instructions on what to expect when I went inside. They were telling me not to worry and be calm. I assured them that I was all right but a little excited about what was about to happen. After I had received all the instructions, they led me to the base of the large central pyramid. There we stood, and suddenly, in total unison, we all chanted a long prayer. When that was completed, a tiny door seemed to open at the base of the pyramid, directly in front of us. One by one, the people bent over and stepped inside. Finally, it was my turn. I bent over and slowly moved inside. It was very dark and quiet. Once inside, the others formed a circle around me and held hands. They chanted for a few seconds, and they began to glow with a soft light. As the chanting continued, even the room began to glow with that same soft light. From beneath my feet, there was a rumble. The ground began to rise slowly upward. The sound of rocks rubbing began to echo in the pyramid, and I began to rise upward. I stepped off the rising section as it rose upward. It stopped, and I looked at it. It was a tomb. Silently, the great stone cover began to rise until it was about eight feet above the ground. When I looked up at the people who came in with me, they had undergone a change. They were no longer flesh but were translucent. Thoughts came into me from the leader. He explained that I was about to undergo an initiation. He said that everyone would have to eventually enter here, and this is what we were preparing ourselves for. Then he told me it was now time. I slowly got into the tomb and lay down. As I felt the cold stone on my back, the cover began to come back down onto the tomb. I lay there as quietly as I could. With a deep and final thud, the cover sealed the tomb. I lay there, closing my eyes. In my heart, there was a loneliness and a feeling of loss. The silence was total, making me lose all sense of being. I was hardly breathing, feeling in tune with the silence. Then somewhere, from deep within me, there was a chant. It was coming from inside but was being reflected from everywhere. I heard and began to become that chant. It was the AUM, the universal tone that we use so often. From that pit of darkness came a blinding light. Brighter and brighter it came, until everything was light. From that point, I kind of rose. There was light, and the place that I was in was made of crystal. The light was everywhere, reflecting off the surfaces of the crystals. As I watched for what seemed like an eternity, the crystals began to communicate with me. What they were giving me was a knowingness, a sense of the totality of my being. It was clear and total. There was no longer anything that was in conflict with anything else. It was all a part of a total symphony, a kind of universal movement that all existed now and forever at the same time. Then, in the smallest speck that was in the middle of my existence, there was a hole in the light. It began to become larger and larger, and I was being drawn into it. The last thing I remembered was that I must fulfill my mission on earth. When I got up, I was shaking. The sun had already risen and I felt totally drawn out. Looking around my bedroom, there was nothing that looked the same. Everything looked new, fresh, and alive. It was as if I never really saw anything before this moment. I felt I was blind until then to the world and its beauty. Even now, there is nothing to compare to what I had that night.

Many people have experienced similar dreams. Perhaps our experiences may not be as earth-shattering as this one was, but they all have the same nature. The level of our experience will depend on where we are on the evolutionary path and how much progress we have made.

7
Examples of
Dream Analysis

The following dreams are actual dreams of friends, relatives, fellow workers, and my students. They were selected because they are typical dreams. All the analyses are mine. A couple of my interpretations were given intuitively, without strictly following the methods in this book. However, the analyses are still similar to what the book method would have disclosed. After I had interpreted a dream, the dreamer and I would discuss the events in his or her life that the dream related to. These situational backgrounds are also provided.

These dreams may be used to practice the techniques given in this book. After reading through a dream, look up the meaning of the universal symbols that have been underlined. Using the symbolic definitions, think how you would analyze the dream. Then compare your results with the ones in the back of the chapter.

Dream analysis does not have concrete answers like mathematics does. It is more akin to a social science, in which general principles and tendencies underlie the answers.

Sample Dreams

Dream 1

happy

tired

confused

◐ In this dream, a <u>baby</u> was given to me by an <u>angel</u>. I thought that this was really fantastic and was very proud of the <u>baby</u>. After a while, the <u>baby</u> began to <u>cry</u> at every little thing. I tried everything to quiet the <u>baby</u>, but it would only stop <u>crying</u> for a short time. One day, there was nothing that I could do to quiet the <u>baby</u>, and I asked <u>God</u> for help. The <u>angel</u> reappeared and said, "Give up." I got up <u>laughing</u>.

Dream 2

anger

tired

◐ I dreamt that I was on a <u>boat</u> heading up a <u>river</u>. The <u>river</u> was very narrow, and there were many over-hanging <u>trees</u>. Suddenly, <u>people</u> jumped from the <u>trees</u> and were trying to take over the <u>boat</u>. I fought them and threw them into the <u>water</u>. But the num-bers of <u>people</u> were endless, and even as I looked ahead, there were more <u>trees</u> and more <u>people</u> wait-ing to jump onto the <u>boat</u>. I then woke up.

Dream 3

tired

◐ I had this dream about this <u>clock</u>. I have a <u>clock</u> on my back that constantly tells me the time. I have many places to go to, by a certain time. I am con-stantly wanting to go to other places, only I never seem to have enough time. I would like to throw away the <u>clock</u>, but it's tied to my back. I cannot re-move the <u>knot</u>.

Dream 4

◐ I dreamt that I was with my <u>grandmother</u>. We were at her <u>house</u>, which was very large. The <u>house</u> was spotlessly clean, but we had to thoroughly clean it, every little corner. When we were through, my <u>grandmother</u> said that we were not finished because the <u>roof</u> was full of dirt. The <u>roof</u> was steep, but she somehow managed to get up there with little trouble and began sweeping it. I helped her <u>sweep</u>, and we then hosed the <u>roof</u> down with <u>water</u>. After the <u>roof</u> was clean, we left the <u>house</u>. While we were gone, the <u>house</u> burned down. My <u>grandmother</u>'s only remark was "It's okay, since the <u>house</u> was clean."

Dream 5

◗ I am living in an under<u>water cave</u>, with the only <u>entrance</u> lying between <u>two</u> large <u>rocks</u>. In the <u>cave</u>, there are many <u>books</u> in a large <u>library</u>. All the <u>furniture</u> is made of <u>stone</u>. I would like to leave the <u>cave</u>, only it's been so long since I've been outside that I am afraid. I wake up feeling very lazy.

Dream 6

◗ I am <u>running</u> in an area that looks like a <u>square</u>. There is no one else that I can see, but I know that only on the <u>points</u> of the <u>square</u> will I be safe. The <u>points</u> are like the <u>bases</u> of a baseball <u>field</u>. I cannot see the other <u>bases</u> when I am on one <u>base</u> because of the <u>fog</u>. Although I am safe on the <u>base</u>, I cannot stay there long.

scared Each time I get to a <u>base</u>, I have to leave. I am getting frantic, trying to be safe and not get caught. I felt tired when I got up in the morning.

Dream 7

◗ I am in a <u>city</u> somewhere. There were many <u>buildings</u>, none of which were more that <u>two</u> stories high. The whole area looked like the <u>slum</u> neighborhood. Someone came out of an <u>alley</u> and began to <u>chase</u> me. I <u>ran</u> and <u>ran</u>, in and out of the back <u>alleys</u> of the <u>city</u>. Finally, I stopped and saw that I had lost the <u>person chasing</u> me. I then wanted to leave this neighborhood but didn't know where to go. I was <u>lost</u>. Every-

tired
and cold

where I went, the <u>buildings</u> all looked the same. There was no <u>direction</u> or street <u>sign</u> that showed me where I was. I felt like giving up.

Dream 8

◐ I was in a <u>large house</u>. It was <u>white</u>, with many expensive pieces of <u>furniture</u>. As I moved through the <u>house</u>, I could hear <u>music</u>. The <u>music</u> was so catchy that you couldn't help but move with it. I was searching for someone, but could not find them. I heard a <u>noise</u> that came from inside the <u>closet</u>. Looking inside, I saw someone hiding in the corner, behind the <u>clothes</u>. I said, "I'm glad that I found you. You don't have to hide anymore." She came out, and I could see that she was very <u>beautiful</u>, only she was dressed in <u>rags</u>.

Dream 9

◐ I am in a large <u>desert</u>, which is covered with <u>sand</u>. There are many <u>dunes</u> and only one spot with <u>water</u>. There are many <u>trees</u> growing around the <u>pool</u>. I am stuck there. I have tried many times to leave. Each time, I cannot find my way and have to return to the <u>oasis</u>.

Dream 10

◐ I am shopping with my <u>daughter</u> in a large <u>market</u>. She wants to buy everything. I keep telling her no, we have to live within our budget. I buy the usual <u>food</u>, but she wants other types of <u>food</u>. She nags and nags. I tell her maybe we can afford to buy them later. She says, "You always tell me that."

Dream 11

◐ I don't remember too many dreams, but this dream had three parts to it. Each seemed separate, yet they related to each other. The first dream was of a <u>lady</u>

with strawberry blond hair. She seemed tall and had her arms overhead, holding a cat. The cat was large, with a shiny gray coat and white tips on her paws. The cat was very beautiful, and the fur was flowing, almost moving in slow motion. The lady had a gray outfit on, which matched the cat, and it too was moving in the same slow, flowing motion as the cat. On top of the gray outfit, she had on a blue, transparent, sheer outer garment with flowers on it.

The second dream was of a large kitchen with white walls. It was a very large room, and it looked new. In the middle of the kitchen was an old booth, with some of my friends in it. I recognized them then, but I don't remember who they are now, only that they were old friends. The booth was totally out of place, and I knew that it had to go.

The third dream was of a large building. It was under construction and only partly completed. It was off-white in color, and the construction used massive beams. It was about twelve stories high, and I had no idea how tall it was going to be. From the front, there were no windows, but I knew that there were windows in the building. The windows must have been on the other side of the building. There was also a road running in front of the building, new, unused, and made of black asphalt. I also had the feeling that the building was to be an office building of some sort.

Analysis of Sample Dreams

Dream 1

Universal Symbols

baby = new beginnings
angel = guide or messenger
crying = emotional release
laughing = releasing tension

Theme

Someone is trying too hard and is missing the point.

Analysis

The person has become interested in something new, something that he has been guided into doing. In the beginning of this new venture, everything seemed to be going well. There was, however, something that was being done incorrectly. This was pointed out to him, but he chose to ignore it. His problem is an emotional attachment to the method of correcting the situation. Real progress will happen once he releases his need to do it his own way. No real effort is required on his part.

Actual Situation

This person had started a new business and had hired some people to work for him. In the beginning, things were going well. Later, problems began to crop up. He has been trying to make changes, but things are not improving. He refuses any advice and seems to blame others for his problems.

Dream 2

Universal Symbols

> boat = ability to pass easily through emotional times
> river = source of life; channel that allows movement through life with minimal conflict
> tree = inexhaustible life
> people = mob = action without thought
> water = emotional consciousness

Theme

People are trying to get into the boat.

Analysis

The dreamer is obviously going through some difficult times with little problem. There are many whom he meets who are not as fortunate as he and are trying to get a free ride with him. He does not want to give anyone a free ride and is trying to straighten out their lives. It is a lot of work on his part, and the people have to go through some difficult emotional times to straighten themselves out. He sees the futility of his action as there is no end of those who want to rely on him. But he is probably going to continue what he is doing as it supports his purpose in life.

Actual situation

The person is doing quite well financially. He is always helping many people, many of whom are members of his family. They always approach him for financial aid, but instead he gives them spiritual and philosophical guidance. He agreed with the analysis and chose to continue doing what he has always done.

Dream 3

Universal Symbols

clock = automaton-like existence
knot = restriction

Theme

Someone is tied down by time.

Analysis

The dreamer is tied to the requirements of his life. Much of his time is being consumed by the demands of a strenuous lifestyle. He dreams of the day when he will be free of the things that must be done so that he can do what he wants to do. He wants to change, but it all seems impossible. The solution is to have someone else help him to free himself from the situation, someone who can see what the problems are (he cannot—symbolically, they are on his back) and guide him.

Actual Situation

The person is an executive and says that he is bored with his lifestyle. He has too many responsibilities to be able to do what he really wants. He says he sees the situation but that there is nothing he can do at this time.

Dream 4

Universal Symbols

    grandmother = loving maternal guardian
    house = self
    roof = limits of thinking
    sweep = to clear or remove a past debt
    water = emotional consciousness
    burned = fire = energy of spiritual transformation

Theme

Someone is ready for change.

Analysis

Parental guidance is allowing the dreamer to become what is being manifested. The large house means that the potential of this person is tremendous and has been with this person from early childhood. The time has come for change and growth to take place. Changes in thinking must come first. Debts owed have been paid, and the emotional attachments have been removed. The energy and ability to move forward are available.

Actual Situation

For many years, this person has limited herself. She was tied to her job and her children, and these have kept her from developing her true potential. A few months after her dream, she changed her direction and became a minister.

Dream 5

Universal Symbols

water = emotional consciousness
cave = concealment and security
entrance = opening = hole = fertility; opening to other
   worlds/levels
two = duality, seeking balance, creation
rock = stone = permanence and harmony
book = record of past and present deeds
library = place to hold records
furniture = personality

Theme

Someone is hiding.

Analysis

The person is withdrawn and hiding from emotional situations. He has free access to the source of his problems within
himself but is too secure within his own little world to change.
He is also very stubborn, too stubborn to see his own problems
and change them.

Actual Situation

The dreamer is outgoing and personable. He seems very nice
but never allows anyone too close to him. He is in his forties
and has never been married or had a serious relationship. He
has no thoughts of changing his lifestyle.

Dream 6

Universal Symbols

running = changes in self
square = lack of balance, unyielding
point = source

base = square = lack of balance, unyielding
field = limitless potential
fog = cloud = concealment, hidden before cleansing
   process

Theme

Someone is being chased.

Analysis

The person is out of balance. He is trying to accomplish many things, only he is really going around in circles. He always has a new goal or a new project that he works at with much energy. When he finally gets into the project, it is a letdown, and he finds something new. He is afraid to stop, just as he is afraid to continue. His solution is to commit himself to something.

Actual Situation

This was a young man who was trying to decide what he should do with his life. He had many talents and was having difficulty choosing a profession.

Dream 7

Universal Symbols

city = patterned living
building = physical self
two = duality, seeking balance, creation
slum = run-down buildings = run-down physical self
alley = path = guided journey
chase = in pursuit of or becoming; avoidance
run = changes in self
person = stranger = lost person
lost = loss = removal to open the way for something new
direction = source of goodness
sign = characteristic of

Theme

Someone was running away and got lost.

Analysis

The person has been living a very structured life. She has a poor image of herself. She is frustrated. There are better things coming, but she is subconsciously resisting them. She has lost sight of the goodness in life. In order to improve her life, she needs solitude to regain direction and more vitality.

Actual Situation

The dreamer is a young woman who has been involved with drugs for a few years. She is beginning to see the fallacy of this path, but has no real direction in solving her predicament.

Dream 8

Universal Symbols

> large house = building = self, with great potential
> white = something coming into being; a reality
> furniture = personality
> music = higher universal form of communication
> noise = confusion
> closet = hidden capabilities
> clothes = personality
> beautiful = purity
> rags = remnants of old personality

Theme

Something hidden has been found.

Analysis

A controlled outward appearance is very important to this person. Her personality has been well cultivated, and she likes it.

Recently though, she has been moving in a different circle. There has been more communication with higher forces. She is becoming a new person, not just outwardly, but inwardly more pure and not tied as much to outer appearances. But with these changes comes confusion. She should just relax and let things run their course.

Actual Situation

This woman has had a rather happy life. She has sufficient funds to get whatever she wants. She dresses well and seems to have everything going for her. Recently, she has been spending a lot of time in prayer, and changes are beginning to occur. Her value system has changed, leaving her feeling unsettled. She has no idea what is going on but is aware of a lot of energy inside of her.

Dream 9

Universal Symbols

desert = a place where transformation without distractions can occur
sand = endless and eternal
dune = hill = small aspiration
water = emotional consciousness
tree = inexhaustible life
pool = lake = mirror of the soul; transition plane to different levels of consciousness
oasis = salvation

Theme

Someone is trapped.

Analysis

The person is very close to a change in her life. She is surrounded by many different possibilities, many things that seem worthwhile to put her efforts into. These are endless in number, and she is continually going after them. The things that she seeks are not too significant. The real goal is right where she is. She has not seen the answer that is within herself. All efforts to find the answer elsewhere will fail, and she will continue to feel alone.

Actual Situation

The dreamer is a "seminar junkie," going from one discipline to another. She has continued this for many years, never seeming to find an answer. All the different classes seem to be what she needs in the beginning, but they later are found to be lacking. She continues to explore other disciplines.

Dream 10

Universal Symbols

>   daughter = a more alive part of self
>   market = ability to choose from many sources
>   food = source of energy

Theme

Someone cannot express inner energy.

Analysis

Person has a conflict within. She has lived in much the same way for most of her life. There is an inner urge to consider different possibilities. There is a feeling that she somehow does not deserve this yet, so she has denied herself opportunity. She may have some kind of health problem (my own intuition).

Actual Situation

This woman has had many health problems in the past. She has had them for a long time and has not received satisfactory results from doctors that she visits. She had thought of other types of treatment but has not done anything yet. She said that she will now consider other options.

Dream 11

Universal Symbols

lady = self
strawberry blond hair = physical and emotional energy
tall = growth (not in dictionary)
arms overhead = activity, moving to a higher level
cat = guardian of marriage and relationships
gray = between black and white = beginning to come into
   being
white = a reality; manifested
beautiful = purity
fur = nature of animal energy
blue = spiritual
flower = in process of change, transition, or growth

kitchen = room = physical self
room = identification of physical body
booth = furniture = personality or aspect of self
friend = different aspect of self

large building = self with great potential
12 = 1+2 = 3 = balance
window = to see beyond one's limitations
road = path = guided journey
black = in process of becoming real
office = central guide (my intuitive impression)

Themes

1. Someone has a slow-moving relationship.
2. Someone has something old that is no longer needed.
3. Someone has a good foundation, but there is more work
to complete.

Analysis

In the first dream, the dreamer has much mental energy. She
holds relationships and marriage in the highest esteem. She is
moving very slowly into a new relationship. It is very rewarding
but has not yet been fully manifested. The white feet of the cat

mean that steps have been taken to fulfill all aspects of the relationship. She is undergoing a spiritual transformation, which has made this new relationship possible. This spiritual transformation is not yet complete and must be given sufficient time.

The second dream is an emotional dream. Emotionally, she has been made new, with much more room for creativity. There is still one remaining hang-up. New energy (from food that can be prepared in the kitchen) is available when the booth, which she no longer needs, is removed. (Psychically I knew that the booth represented stores that she owned.) The dreamer holds on to her business for others and not for herself. But these are out of place in her new life.

The third dream deals with the physical self. The woman has made progress physically and psychologically. There are still more physical changes that will be happening, but they are almost completed. The dreamer has many abilities to help herself and others. Since there are no windows on the front of the building, it indicates she is keeping herself away from the public. The knowledge of windows means that there is someone in close contact with the dreamer that few know about. The way is clear, but it is too early to start on her mission. Soon what she is to do will become clear. She is a catalyst, making things happen around her. She is the force that brings them into being.

Actual Situation

The woman has been recently divorced and has found someone new. She is very much in love with the new person but has had some difficulty getting the relationship going. Some commitments have been made, but more time will be required to develop the relationship.

She also owns three stores, which she has held for a number of years. She has kept them because they gave her independence and she wanted future jobs for her children. Her children have moved on and are no longer interested in working in the stores. She had just decided to sell these businesses the night that she had the dreams.

She has been on the spiritual path for the past seven years. She has made much progress with her physical self, although she is still working to improve it. She has been in semiseclusion for the past three months trying to get her financial and mental worlds in order. She has plans to get involved with many different things and work with other people to help them on their spiritual journies.

8

How to Dream
Constructively

We have great potential that could be realized if the deeper levels of our minds could be used. It has been estimated that even those considered geniuses use no more than ten percent of the total capability of the human mind. What if there was a way to make more use of the unused portions of the mind and do it while sleeping? Impossible? Hardly. It is not only possible, it is already being done by everyone, to a greater or lesser extent every day.

My first conscious experience with the additional capabilities of the mind occurred quite by accident. Cramming may not be the best method to prepare for college exams, but almost all of us have probably done so. There were too many occasions when I just didn't seem to have sufficient time to go through everything. Just before going to sleep, I would review a single page of notes that I kept for each subject. During the short night, my dreams would work on all the problems that I had experienced during the semester. Over and over I would review the entire text, solving problems that I had not been able to do earlier and arriving at the correct solution. I would wake in the morning with a clear understanding of the subject. I would say to my family, "Don't even talk to me, I have all the answers in my head," as I would head for school to face the exam. There was a drawback to this method: the information acquired during the night would begin to fade, although not quite as quickly as my dreams did after waking. But the method worked adequately enough since it got me a degree in electrical engineering. After college, I forgot about the technique because I had no further use for learning during my sleep.

As my interest in the spiritual/psychic field began to increase, I once again began to delve into the possibilities that opened up during sleep. Remembering my experiences in college, I began to outline what had occurred. Combining this with my knowledge of parapsychology, I found that *desire directs dreams*. This led to the following process that creates the proper environment for constructive dreaming.

Clearing the Mind

The first step is to *clear the mind of the events of the day*. Even without attempting constructive dreaming, this is a good practice. In clearing the mind, we are not attempting to remove events from our memory. This is virtually impossible. Once a memory is implanted into the mind, it remains forever. But, what we can do is remove some of the strong emotional charge associated with a given memory. Fortunately, most of our daily experiences have little or no emotion tied to them. When troublesome events do happen, however, we must be able to handle them.

Significant events are the easiest to clear. They are the easiest to remember and work with. An argument with the boss that resulted in a shouting match or a near accident during rush hour are easily recalled. But we may also have subtle problems, and these are more difficult to identify. Each small problem, taken by itself, appears insignificant. However, if they keep recurring, they can grow into significant problems. Examples of these include someone always parking in your stall at work, the newspaper boy repeatedly throwing the paper into the hedge, or the children never remembering to put away their toys. When these little repetitive problems are also cleared, the quality of our dreams and sleep will greatly improve. They reflect our state of mind and the quality of our lives.

The clearance can be done at any time but is usually most beneficial just prior to going to sleep. To begin, sit comfortably with your eyes closed. Begin to breathe slowly and quietly, allowing your body to relax. It is best not to lie down while doing this. Lying down, being relaxed, and having closed eyes are too suggestive of sleep and may make you fall asleep before you can finish your clearance.

Once you get comfortable, begin to review all the events of the day, beginning with the first thing you remember when waking. Go over each event, looking for anything that may have an emotional reaction tied to it. Even the most simple things, like the neighbor's dog barking early in the morning or the phone ringing during a nap, may have triggered an emotional reaction. Once such an event is recalled, review it completely and try to see what actually caused the problem. In most cases, the cause is not the incident itself, but its constant repetition. Now forgive the other party or parties for their involvement in the incident. Of course, we are also guilty for allowing the incident to become an incident. We must also forgive ourselves for our part. This process of review and forgiveness continues until the whole day has been covered.

Remain seated with closed eyes and become aware of the thoughts and images that come to mind. The seemingly automatic rambling of the mind is actually a process of reviewing events out of the past. Now clear the mind of the incidents of your past. As these flash before your mind's eye, acknowledge each incident and again forgive everyone, including yourself. Do not allow yourself to become emotionally tied to any incident. Let the emotions fade away. Continue this process for about ten minutes. The time limit is necessary or you may find yourself doing this all night.

Programming the Mind

You are now ready to *program the mind to work on a specific problem*. Continue to sit quietly until you feel calm and relaxed. At this point, there is a fine balance between the outer and inner levels of the mind. It is possible for our conscious level of mind to communicate directly with our subconscious mind. An affirmative statement will direct the dream that will be worked on during the night. Each of the three types of dreams (physical/emotional clearance, spiritual guidance, and psychic experience), has a different role and a different type of programming is required.

Programming for a Physical/Emotional Problem Clearance

For the most part, there is little you need to do to program yourself for physical/emotional problem clearance. This occurs naturally whenever you fall asleep. There are instances, however, when you may want to use the programming technique. Suppose you have a specific problem, such as one with a mother-in-law, that you need to release. You will find the following programming technique very useful. During the quiet that exists just before you fall asleep, read the following statement aloud with feeling:

> I am about to fall asleep. During my sleep, I will experience my problem with _____ that is limiting my aliveness now. I want to experience that problem completely, understanding all its ramifications. I will then release the problem from my life. I will make all necessary changes to prevent the reactivation of this problem in my life.

In the morning, record your dream immediately. Its message should be obvious. It will describe the problem and provide a solution. It is not important if you are unable to extract the message. The problem is already being released from your life.

The effectiveness of this technique is illustrated by a young man who came to me with a problem. It seems he had difficulty with a project he was trying to complete. He had been working on it for some time when he came for help. When asked if he would like to try to solve his own problem on a higher level of consciousness, he quickly consented. The technique was given to him, and he promised to try it that night. A few weeks later, he returned with his dream recorded and reported the following:

● When I saw you the last time, I didn't tell you what my problem was. It had to do with my business, where I have a few people working for me. There were so many things that had to be done and so little time to do them in. I thought I was going to go crazy trying to do them all. That's when I came to you for help. When you gave me the instructions for programming, I tried it out that night. I didn't know what to expect. The next morning when I got up, I was really tired. You know the feeling, like you're dying. My whole body was sore. But as soon as I got up, I remembered my dream and quickly wrote it down. What I saw was so simple, I couldn't believe it.

This was my dream: I was planting a garden. I had bought the best little vegetable seeds that I could find in the store. I prepared the ground well and planted the little seeds. Each morning, I would wake up and notice that the plants weren't growing as well as I thought they should. So I got out into the garden and pulled the plants up to check the roots to see why the plants weren't growing. Seeing that the roots looked okay, I would replace the plants into the ground."

I think I have it figured out. I have the right people and the right preparation. All I have to do is to let things alone long enough so that things can develop as they should. I did that. Well, not totally. I quietly looked over everyone's shoulders, giving compliments whenever they made progress. And it seems to be working. It's coming together, and we're going to make it.

It is wonderful to see someone make greater use of their capabilities. With the aid of dream analysis, this person had identified his problem and obtained his solution. He is now on his

way to claiming more of the natural abilities that most of us
have forgotten that we have.

Programming for Spiritual Guidance

Another type of programming is for spiritual guidance. For
maximum benefit, we should be working toward spiritual progress on the conscious level. Experience indicates that if we are
not, we tend to receive only a simple message. But if we are
working diligently on our spiritual development and are now in
need of further guidance, the messages of the dreams tend to be
very significant. In either case, the following programming
statement can be used:

> I have been working on my spiritual development. At this
> moment, I am in need of spiritual guidance to help me be-
> come more balanced. I need the key that will help me un-
> lock the door to more awareness and aliveness. When I
> awake, I will remember this key and be able to use it to
> make progress spiritually. I know that all outer efforts will
> be supported by inner progress.

When you have a spiritual guidance dream, analyze it to extract the message. Then you need to act upon the guidance received. The subconscious mind is like a little child. If we
receive our guidance and ignore it, it may be a while before another significant piece of information is provided. We cannot lie
to our inner intelligence. It is aware of everything that is happening and makes appropriate changes immediately. If action is
not taken, it realizes that we are not sincere and refuses to provide any more spiritual guidance.

If the programming does not work the first time, don't be discouraged. All of our efforts to gain balance and spiritual growth
are noted by our inner intelligence. Nothing positive ever goes
unrewarded, just as nothing negative ever goes unpunished.
Everything we do will be abundantly returned to us. In the case
of dreams, all positive efforts will result in more balance, awareness, and vitality.

Programming the Psychic Experience

Psychic experiences are usually attempted by those who are curious about a future or past event. When trying to have a psychic experience, prepare yourself in the same way as above. Once you have cleared the day's activities, wait until you feel a calmness. Then read the following:

> I have released the problems that occupy my conscious life. I am interested in *(person/place/thing)*. I am prepared to enter into a deeper level of consciousness, one free of the limitations of time and space. There I will experience the true essence of my being, seeing things as they really are. With all that I experience, I will recall clearly the things that are most important or beneficial to me at this moment.

After saying this, let yourself drift off to sleep. The technique is more effective the less time you spend thinking or moving around between the programming statement and sleep.

Be prepared for whatever happens. Penetrating the time/space barrier will open you to the limitless possibilities that exist. The programming will cause your dream to focus on whatever you are most interested in. Remember that the primary purpose of the psychic dream is to prepare you for the future. What is seen may appear to be negative, such as a death or an accident. On the other hand, it may be very positive, such as a beautiful and joyous occasion or a future lover. Whatever it is, it is not fixed and impossible to change. It is up to you to do what you want with this information.

9
Dream Analysis
to Increase
Your Psychic Ability

As we progress in dream analysis, we may use this ability to help others by analyzing their dreams. It will become apparent that the normal method of interpreting dreams is sometimes insufficient. In some dreams, the dreamer only remembers a part of the dream or some sketchy details. In these cases, it is almost impossible to give an accurate interpretation. No analysis is possible until the missing details can be provided. The psyche can be used to fill in the missing pieces. For most people, however, the psyche has long been inactive within the depths of the mind. The exercises in this chapter will begin to reactivate it.

To illustrate the use of psychic ability, let me relate the shortest dream I have had to interpret. In one of my classes, a woman wanted her dream analyzed. "I dreamt of the number ninety-six. That's all, just ninety-six." I asked her if she remembered any colors or had any feelings. She repeated that she only remembered the number ninety-six. My mind quickly raced back to numerology and reduced ninety-six $(9+6)$ to fifteen $(1+5)$ to six. I could only recall that the number six was an emotional/mental number and possibly had something to do with healing. Taking a deep breath, I cleared my mind.

"Well, that's not much to go on," I said, as I began to reach deep within my mind. Finally, after what seemed an eternity, I began to speak and was amazed at what I heard myself saying.

This problem deals with a relationship that is about to break up. You and your husband or boyfriend are now heading in different directions, and it's time for you to go your separate ways. You are aware that this is happening, but your boyfriend is not. The decision is of an emotional nature, and the problem exists primarily in your mind. In other words, you are thinking of ending the relationship, based on the gut feelings you have about it. It's difficult for you to pinpoint the problem other than that it should end. There is still hope for the relationship, but it requires a lot of work from both of you. I don't see this taking place. What I do see is that you will probably be with this person for a length of time yet, in spite of your feelings and your thoughts of leaving him. This is due to the fear you have of not having anyone. Your fears are understandable, for he is your security, and coping with life is difficult. The decision is yours and only you can make the choice.

"How did you do that?" she asked, reflecting my own feelings. "You know, I think you're right. I've been thinking that my boyfriend and I no longer communicate. Only I don't know what to do about it. I'll have to think about this more."

The analysis had hit close to home. It allowed her to recognize a problem. What she chose to do from that point on was her decision. This example shows how we can use the psychic level of mind to help others. It allows us to get past outer appearances and see the real cause of any problem. It also enables us to empathize with the other person. Suddenly we are able to experience the world from another person's viewpoint.

The awakening of the psyche and its subsequent use is the main theme of all religious and spiritual pursuits. This is true of Christianity, in spite of some denials. The psyche, which is the Greek word for "soul," is a natural part of each one of us. It is at this soul level of mind that real communication begins. This does not mean that there is little value in the normal forms of communication. These have their place at the outer functional levels. But when we are trying to communicate with another on a deeper, more meaningful level, more is needed than words and gestures. What is needed is inner feeling and a meeting of our hearts. It is only in this deeper communion that real communication and the real nature of people can be experienced.

In order to activate the psyche, we must first ask what distorts our ability to see and experience clearly. After all, everything seen or experienced is exactly what it is. But somehow, everything that we experience becomes distorted. For most of us, this distortion cannot be caused by our five senses. They simply record what is out there. So the distortion must occur between the sensory input into the brain and subsequent recall of the original stimulus. Therefore, the distortion must occur within the mind itself. Obviously, our opinions, prejudices, ideals, and attitudes affect what we experience. With these we judge the value of each experience. When an experience is being processed, the mind compares it with others in our memory bank. It then gives it a value on a relative scale. The scale measures positive or negative, right or wrong, high or low. So instead of having a neutral experience, we have reevaluated it relative to others in our life. We now have in our memory a pseudo experience, a mere shadow of the real one.

So nothing new is really experienced, not even a beautiful sunset. Instead of seeing a sunset, the mind is comparing it with others it has experienced in the past. The mind makes a value judgment, calling the sunset more beautiful than a few but maybe not as beautiful as some others.

In the same way, people we meet are compared to others we have known. The comparison may or may not be made consciously, but it happens anyway. The mind quickly notes the new person's mannerisms and appearance, which are then compared with those of other people we know. A value judgment of the new person is instantly made and will bias all future experiences with that person. The new person will be measured as being better than so-and-so, not as smart as so-and-so, almost as good looking as so-and-so, etc. There is no reality, just a lot of comparisons that have nothing to do with this new relationship. So the other person is never really experienced.

By activating our psyche, it becomes possible for us to clearly experience again. We will be able to release the bias that keeps us from experiencing reality. This process of releasing the bias of the mind is called meditation.

Meditation

Meditation is widely misunderstood. It is an ancient practice, which has evolved from many different traditions and customs. In order to understand what it is, meditation must first be seen for what it is not. Meditation is not "programming." Regardless of how much higher new programmed ideals may be, they are still mental creations. A bias will still exist to color our experience of reality. This bias has to be completely removed. Meditation is also not the act of being repeatedly told something or saying something over and over. "Jesus Christ is my Lord and Savior," and "Hail Mary," are programming phrases used by many Christians. Other religions have their own. "Hare Krishna, Hare Krishna, Hare Rama, Hare Rama," "Allah be praised," "Om Mani Padmi Om," "Namu Amidabutsu," are some common meditation chants. These are also called mantras or prayers and are used to calm and still the mind. The benefit derived from chanting comes from its hypnotic effect. Long repetition causes the mind to shut out the world around the would-be meditator. The sound or chant becomes the single point of concentration and does provide some physiological and psychological benefits. In spite of these benefits, this is still not meditation. Real meditation does not begin until all the chanting and prayers end.

It is also clear that meditation is not a certain pose or posture the meditator must assume. Sitting in a full lotus, with the legs crossed and no back support is nearly impossible for all except the young or one trained in yoga. Yet these positions are very important in some schools of meditation.

Finally, meditation is not the process of stopping the mind from thinking. This is similar to someone yelling in a crowded room for everyone to be quiet. The person yelling is not part of the solution but has become part of the problem. The would-be meditator who uses the mind in order to stop thinking is only fooling himself. The mind that is trying to control itself into being quiet is itself a noisy mind. All efforts to become quiet will result in more mental movement. Thinking about controlling the mind is not the solution. It is actually the problem.

Therefore, we can conclude that meditation is neither mantras, postures, nor forced silence. Since meditation is none of these, we can begin to close in on what meditation really is. It is a process of releasing what we already are. We need only to become quiet, to release the hold our thinking mind has on us. In the silence that follows, we can unleash our ability to communicate with our own psyche. We are able to transcend the known and venture into the unknown. An adventure that is vibrant, ever-changing, and unique for each individual.

Several conditions will help us prepare for meditation. First, we need to sit comfortably and relax. Being uncomfortable can become a distraction and has to be corrected. For most westerners, this means sitting in a comfortable chair. Dining room chairs are often best, because they have straight backs. If a chair makes us slouch, we may have a slight difficulty in breathing, which will also distract us. As mentioned earlier, we should not try to meditate while lying down as we will probably just fall asleep. It is said that master teachers can meditate in this position, but since most of us are not masters yet, it is best to leave this position for the future.

Tight clothing, jewelry, the temperature or humidity of the room, noises, and smells can all be distractions that should be eliminated or minimized. Anything that stimulates our senses of sight, smell, hearing, and touch should be controlled. It is difficult to meditate with the smell of bread baking or the loud beat of rock music. With practice, these will have no effect on our meditation. In the beginning, however, we should try to create as positive an environment as we can for our meditation sessions.

While sitting comfortably, allow your eyes to close naturally. There must not be any urgency to do anything. Simply relax and allow things to happen. After your eyes have closed, begin to feel your breathing. Do not attempt to do anything, simply be aware of what is happening. If there is any tightness in the body, stretch or yawn to relieve the tension. Many of the asanas or postures of hatha yoga were initially developed to allow the body to relax.

You will probably have many thoughts and mental images. Make no effort to suppress or get rid of these. Just become aware of them and let them pass. Eventually, the movements of the mind will end, and silence will unfold. That is all there is to it. Until then, the mind is in a struggle with itself.

Most people find it difficult to enter into the silence. Why? Because we are afraid. For our mind to become silent, thinking has to end. Within our subconscious mind is a belief that thinking is life. As Descartes, the French philosopher assserted: "I think, therefore I am." We believe that if we stop thinking, we will cease to exist. This is our fear. It goes unnoticed because it is hidden deep within our subconscious mind. But only *when thinking ends can real meditation begin*. This form of meditation is not very common in the world. In the East, it is called "meditation without seed."

A more common form of meditation is called "meditation with seed." This type of meditation is just what the name implies, it requires a seed, or an object. The object is used to help in concentration. Anything can be used. Staring at a candle, or watching the waves on a lonely beach are common forms of seed meditation. Chanting, singing, or listening to bells toll are also forms of this type of meditation. Whatever the activity, it must be repeated regularly over a long period of time. We continue it until we become tired of watching the candle, chanting the mantra, or dancing the Sufi dance. When we reach this state, transcendental meditation begins.

For most people who are just beginning to meditate, practice should not last for longer than twenty to thirty minutes.

Attitude

When entering into meditation, attitude is important. As the psyche blossoms and our inner energies strengthen, it becomes easier to send and receive energy that exists at all levels. The rule has always been *like attracts like*. Having a negative attitude will begin to attract negative thoughts and experiences into our lives. We will begin to attract people who are feeling down or have many problems. We will begin to identify with these people, and a feeling of pessimism will begin to grow. All kinds of events will begin or continue to go wrong in our lives. So we must *keep a positive attitude*. A positive attitude will create a positive and supportive environment. Everything around us will begin to improve.

A word of caution about doing a psychic reading is appropriate here. We should *never attempt to do a psychic reading on ourselves*. When first tuning into ourselves, we may not experience any problems. Later, when attempting to do a reading for someone else, a problem may come to the surface. While doing the reading, we may suddenly become aware that the reading we are giving sounds a lot like ourselves. We begin to question whom it is we are reading, the other person or ourselves. From this point on, we will always have doubts about our accuracy. Our effectiveness as a psychic will be severely inhibited. If you have to have a reading done, exchange services with another psychic friend.

Practice

Doing dream interpretation for friends is a good way of gaining experience tapping into the psyche. When asked, most people are eager to have their dreams analyzed. These sessions can be mutually beneficial since your friends have a chance to gain some insight into their own inner guidance while you gain experience. Before starting, explain that it is only a practice session. You do not need any extra pressure from the expectations of others.

On your first attempt at a psychic reading, it is nice to have a fallback position. The techniques given in this book can provide this support. Memorizing the more common symbols and typical dreams will give you sufficient information about any dream. Confidence comes with time and practice. Once you have completed the basic analysis of a dream, it is time to reach deep within. Remember the requirements to activate the psyche. Take a deep breath, become calm and relaxed, and allow your mind to clear itself of thoughts. Closing your eyes or focusing your eyes above and behind the person may be helpful. During this brief period, which often seems quite long, a picture may appear in your mind's eye, or a voice may be heard. Be sure to tell the person what you are sensing. Do not suppress anything, thinking that the information may be wrong. Say it! If it is not said, the channel of information may close again and may not reopen for a long time. Watch the dreamer's reactions to be sure that he is getting the message. If you remain calm and quiet, more information may come in. You will have tapped into the psyche. It is possible to receive much information, perhaps a different angle on the situation at hand.

A word of caution is necessary here. Never take any information given as the absolute truth. Always listen to the information, but apply some common sense to what has been received. Too many times, people in the occult or charismatic groups take psychic information as the gospel and may find themselves in trouble. If the information makes sense and seems right for the occasion, by all means use it. But if it does not, think about it, and even discuss it with others. If it still does not feel right, just discard it. We always have free will. We can still make whatever choices we desire.

The development of the psyche is the first step in the evolution of man. It holds the promise of wonder and wisdom. It is important to remember that the psychic level is only one step in the ladder of life. Ultimately, it is a key to even higher levels of awareness. Once this key has served its purpose, it will be put aside to be replaced by other and more wonderful abilities.

10

Creative Dreaming: Building a New Reality

As mentioned earlier, our lives affect our dreams, and our dreams will affect our lives. Everything that happens to us will cause changes in our dreams. Every action we take, every thought we have create a new reality for us. But it is our feelings that give power to our actions. How we choose to live our lives determines what we dream about. This is easy to understand. On the other hand, the idea that dreams can change our lives is more esoteric. To understand this further, let us delve deeper into what is real.

Jesus said that if we just think about doing a sin, the sin has already been committed. In other words, whatever thoughts we may have become part of our reality, even though they seem to be on a different level of reality. He also said, as above, so below. So whatever happens on another level of reality is also happening on the physical plane. Like thoughts, dreams exist on another level of reality. So we must ask whether or not it is possible to change a dream and thereby change reality. If the answer is no, then there is no need to investigate further. If it is yes, then a vast and potent opportunity arises.

In order to change our dreams, we must have free will. This has been ordained as a human prerogative. Each of us is endowed with the power to change anything and everything within our realm of reality, provided we have the desire to do so. Free will, or our ability to choose, is under the direct control of our minds. Through our thoughts, we are able to direct whatever we wish or desire to create. With our emotions, we are able to tap into the innermost capabilities of the mind. The mind simply points the way, and reality follows it.

Our dreams arise from the deeper levels of our mind, but they still exist and function within the conscious mind. Therefore, as part of our great potential, it would seem only natural that whatever we experience in our dreams is also integrated into our reality. Thoughts, mental images, and feelings flow through our many dreams and move to create a new reality. In a continual action-reaction cycle, our life evokes dreams to solve our problems. Then, our dreams form a new reality based on our problem-solving dreams.

Eastern Techniques to Control Dreams

With this background, we are ready to go one step further. We ask if it is possible to *consciously* create a new reality through dreams. This, in fact, has been practiced in certain Eastern schools of mental training for thousands of years. A student is required to practice until he is able to maintain his conscious awareness during his dreams. Next, he is required to experience and understand that there is no difference between the real world and the world of dreams. What he experiences in his dream world is only an extension of his real world. Then, he must learn to control the world of his dreams. Control does not only mean being able to move in his dream at will. It means being in full command. He can do whatever he desires. He can orchestrate the activity in his dream, moving and creating to his heart's content. His instructor may require him to do some impossible tasks. In order to accomplish these, he may perform deeds of magic or enlist the aid of other mystical techniques. He may accomplish these deeds of almost insurmountable difficulty through the use of his mental and physical abilities. Finally, he may be required to do deeds of great heroism, deeds that even endanger himself. All this is required of the student in order to control his destiny and carry his dream experience into the real world.

Traditionally, this type of training requires dedicated practice by a student. Over the years, we have found that the control of dreams is not very difficult. It requires only two things, energy and purposeful effort. Having energy is not very difficult. It requires a sensible lifestyle including proper exercise and rest, good nutrition, and a calm mind. Just what grandmother always recommended.

Purposeful Effort

Purposeful effort is, perhaps, a little more difficult. Consciousness during a dream cannot be achieved through direct effort. Any conscious effort to maintain awareness while falling asleep is doomed to failure. Awareness and falling asleep are mutually exclusive states. It is just impossible to be aware and fall asleep at the same time. Nevertheless, awareness is needed while dreaming in order to make a purposeful effort to make changes in a dream.

While awareness cannot be taken into a dream state, awareness is possible in the middle of a dream. If we have the desire to become aware during our dream, our inner intelligence will make it possible. This may occur accidentally in the midst of the dream. We may notice something that is not right. Perhaps the color of our car is wrong or our watch is on the wrong hand. When we notice it, we realize that we are dreaming. Even though these seem subtle, there are also occasions when the indication is impossible to miss, such as an event that defies natural law, like walking on water. Each individual must program his own trigger mechanism.

There is nothing special about biting one's tongue, but this works for me. Attempting to bite my tongue, a task I find impossible, triggers awareness within my dream. Suddenly I am not hindered by the limitations of matter, time, or space. I may fly like an eagle or travel to strange and distant lands. I may venture into the depths of space, moving through places beyond comprehension. I feel almost like a spirit, capable of making and changing the very essence of life.

While in this state, I usually have a wonderful sense of a different kind of consciousness. It is a consciousness that is best described as transcendental. There is such a heightened state of awareness, such a feeling of euphoria, that words fail to describe it adequately.

In order to enter into this state, it is necessary that the direction of the experience be indicated before going to bed. On several occasions, I have become aware of being aware within a dream. But I did not have the necessary energy to do anything about it. I simply went back to sleep. Thus purposeful effort requires energy, mental purpose, and follow-through.

Programming

The best way of gaining awareness during a dream is through a programming process. The method is similar to the programming methods discussed earlier. Just before going to bed, repeat the following emphatically:

> I am an aware being. I am able to be aware at any time. When I fall asleep, I will fall asleep naturally. As I dream during the night, I shall become aware that I am dreaming. I shall then become fully conscious of this dream state. During this state, I shall be able to do whatever I wish. This I know to be true and shall manifest this in my life. During this night, I wish to experience _____. When I am experiencing this, I wish to change it in this manner: _____.

Then just let yourself fall asleep, and let nature take its course. The results have startled a few who were not expecting this to work. Their description of what happened is usually a series of revelations, in which they were able to experience things far beyond what they ever thought possible. Some were able to work with problems and change the outcome to what they desired. But enough said on this subject. Experience is the best teacher. We enter alone into the silent yet action-filled world of the transcendental. We experience what is right for us. And when we do, we never forget it.

The whole process usually flows easily and smoothly. The programming will help to support the real purpose of this exercise. The changes we desire are usually worked on almost automatically. We are now able to move from the ordinary into a new world of possibilities in our lives.

Love and light be with you always.

Dictionary of Universal Symbols

abandon: To lose touch with the purpose of life; to feel forsaken.

abnormal: To feel rather than to think.

absolute: Perfect, complete.

academy: See "school."

accident: To place responsibility on others.

acid: Active agent in a reaction or relationship.

acrobat: One who is in the process of reversal, especially aging.

actor: See "occupation."

Adam: Perfect male, before corruption.

air: Thoughts; creative energy.

air force: See "armed forces."

airplane: Ability to rise above.

aisle: See "path."

album: See "book."

alchemy: See "chemistry."

alcohol: Creative or destructive energy (depending on use).

alien: Having a different belief system.

alley: See "path."

alpha and omega: Birth and death.

alphabet: Symbols of communication. Also see "symbols."

aluminum: See "metal."

ambidextrous: Versatile; both practical and intuitive.

amethyst: See "gem."

amputate: Removal of restriction.

ancestors: Attributes from the past.

ancestry: Related to the past.

angel: Guide (inner force); messenger.

animal: Having animalistic characteristics. Reluctance to change.

ant: Small and petty.

anvil: Stability, unmoving.

apology: Recognition of error.

apple: Desires or indulgence of desires.

apron: To deny sexuality.

Aquarius: Person concerned with truth.

architect: See "occupation."

Aries: Person concerned with self.

ark: Ability to persevere all hardships.

arm: See "body."

armed forces: Indicates conflict.
  Army: Physical conflict
  Navy: Emotional conflict
  Air Force: Mental conflict

armor: Protection.

army: See "armed forces."

arrow: Source of power.

art: Expressed creativity.

artificial: To disguise; results through use of force.

ash: Total destruction.

aspirin: See "medicine."

astronomer: See "occupation."

attic: Highest level of mind.

aura: Nature or essence of.

Physical Colors
  Red: Physical life energy, strength, vigor
  Orange: Courage, valor, vitality, consideration
  Red-orange: Passion, boldness, honor, loyalty
  Red-violet: Endurance, strength (inner), bravery
  Rose: Serenity, harmony, patience, humility
  Fire-orange: Ability to give physical healings (especially with hands)
  Golden-orange: Cleansed body, transmutation of negativity

Emotional Colors
  Blue: Faith, trust, religious beliefs, piety
  Violet: Searching, spiritually awakened, devotional, artistic

  Blue-violet: Inspirational, peace, forgiveness, spirituality
  Blue-green: Highly artistic, selfless, on the path
  Emerald-green: Highly creative healing ability
  Indigo: Mystic
  Purple: Dedicated service to humanity

Mental Colors
  Yellow: Joyous, friendly, learns easily, bright
  Green: Balanced, sincerity, intelligent searcher
  Yellow-orange: Trustworthy, ability to use creative imagination
  Yellow-green: Adaptable, positive thinking, highly creative imagination
  Gold: Ability to tap into Universal Mind through meditation
  Turquoise: High-level healer, mental healer
  Lime: Wisdom, enlightenment

Spiritual Colors
  Indigo: Searching for truth, dedicated, mystical
  Ultra-turquoise: Ability to give spiritual healings, work on the inner planes
  Translucent turquoise: Purity, no attachment to physical universe
  Cosmic white light: Perfection, oneness, beingness

Negative Colors
  Brown: Too earthy, animalistic
  Rusty brown: Egocentric, carnal
  Red-brown: Depraved, perverse, abnormal

Brown-orange: Repressed, no ambition, lazy
Coral-brown: Fearful, unsure
Pink: Immaturity an adult
Salmon: Heartbreak
Orchid: Undecided, fanciful
Fuchsia: Sorrowful, unfulfilled
Mustard: Deceitful, weak-willed, liar
Gray: Illness
Black: Fatal illness
No color: Impending death
automobile: See "vehicle."
autumn: See "seasons."
axe: Power of knowledge.
baby: New beginnings.
bag: See "basket."
bait: See "lure."
ball: Completion or an ending.
bandages: Protection, especially during periods of change.
banner: See "flag."
barn: Holding back animal instincts.
barrier: Restriction.
base (alkaline): Passive agent in a reaction or relationship.
base (bottom or foundation): Beliefs.
basement: Sexual identification; inhibitions and restrictions.
basket: Womb; protection until the time for manifestation.
bath: Cleansing; regeneration and purification.
baton: See "staff."
battle: See "fight."
bear: Person who is cruel and crude.
beauty: Purity.
bee: Organization and industry.
bell: Creative power being released; to transform; the ability to cause changes.
belly: See "body."

belt: Moral virtue.
bicycle: See "vehicle."
bird: Spiritual aspirations; ability to rise above.
birth: New beginnings. (See chapter 6.)
black: See "color."
blanket: Security and protection.
blood: Sacrifice.
blue: See "color."
boat: Ability to pass easily through emotional times; spiritual vehicle.
body: Self.
  Hair: Energy (depending where on body)
  Head: Mental ability
  Skull: Limits of thinking
  Eyes: Door to real (inner) self
  Face: Personality
  Mouth: Destructive (devour) or creative (speech) ability
  Teeth: Expression of activity
  Neck: Will or self-restriction
  Skin: Protection
  Shoulder: Carrier of labor
  Lungs: Source of spiritual energy
  Heart: Source of love
  Solar plexus: Source of healing
  Stomach: Inner transformation
  Belly: Source of power
  Spine: Major energy channel within the body
  Tailbone: Source of energy
  Arm and hand: Activity, to move higher or lower
  Genitals: To recreate
  Leg: Ability to change direction or path
  Foot: Support and foundation
bolt: See "lock."
bone: Inner strength.
bonnet: See "hat."

book: Record of past and present deeds.

boot: See "footwear."

bottle: Salvation.

boulder: See "rock".

boundary: Self-made limitations in life.

bow (and arrow): Life force.

bowl: See "cup."

box: The subconscious.

branch: See "grass."

breath: To assimilate spiritual power.

breathing (heavy): Release of emotional conflict.

bridge: Opening or link to new awareness.

broom: See "brush."

brush: To clear or remove.

buckle: Self-defense and protection.

bubble: Completion; protection for whatever it surrounds.

Buddha: High being teaching wisdom and virtue.

building: Self, as related to physical body and mental identification. Each floor is a different level of awareness, higher floors being higher levels. Also see "basement" and "attic."

bulb: See "seed."

bull: Animal superiority; father symbol.

bunch: Sacrifice.

burn: See "fire."

butterfly: Transformation.

button: See "fastener."

cable: See "rope."

caduceus: Self-healing.

camel: Process of change is helped by being alone.

camouflage: Putting on an act for others.

cancer (disease): Physical ailment due to inner tension.

Cancer: Person concerned with emotional relationships.

candelabra: Spiritual light and salvation.

candle: Individual light and guidance from within.

canopy: Good luck and protection.

canyon: See "crevice."

cap: See "hat."

Capricorn: Person concerned with action.

car: See "vehicle."

carpenter: See "occupation."

carrier: Messenger.

cask: Preservation.

castle: Spiritual power.

cat: Guardian of marriage and relationships.

catalyst: Transformer and stimulus.

catastrophe: Sudden transformation.

cauldron: Germination.

cave: Concealment and security.

ceiling: Accepted upper limit.

cemetery: Record of past growth and changes.

censor: Inner wisdom and guidance.

Centaur: Domination by baser forces.

center: Source or Creator.

chain: Bonding or holding something together.

chair: Support.

chalice: See "cup."

chamber: See "vault."

chant: To bring into attunement.

chaos: Confusion.

chase: In pursuit of or becoming. (See Chapter 6.)

chef: See "occupation."

chemistry: Transformation process or method.

cherubim: Religion; vigilance.

chest: See "body."

child: To become simple and trusting again.
choice: Crossroads; two balancing, opposing forces.
Christ: High being teaching love.
chrome: See "metal."
church: Inner search for truth.
circle: Unity; perfection in man.
circumference: See "boundary."
city: Patterned living, which limits or eliminates choices; to be without freedom.
clasp: See "fastener."
class: Obtaining new knowledge. (See Chapter 6.)
clerk: See "occupation."
climate: Indicates individual's outlook.
  Sunny: Peaceful
  Raining: Anticipating change
  Cloudy: Quiet before the storm (change)
  Windy: Energetic
  Cold: Unloving and selfish
  Warm: Loving and giving
cloak: Veil to hide behind; to display position.
clock: Automaton-like existence (living like a robot).
closet: Hidden capabilities.
clothes: Personality.
cloud: Concealment; hidden before cleansing process.
clover: Balanced.
clown: Opposite of "king." Also see "fool."
club: To force into submission.
coal: Latent energy.
coat: See "cloak."
cobweb: Complex living.
coffin: Preparation for change or rebirth.
cold: Solitude; unloving.
collar: Restriction of will.
color: Characteristic. Also see "aura."

Red: Physical; energy and power
Orange: Emotional; feeling and healing
Yellow: Mental; thinking and energy
Green: Healing; peace and calm
Blue: Spiritual; religion and universal love
Purple: Inspiration; royalty and wisdom
Violet: Unity; possibilities
White: A new reality manifesting; coming into being
Black: Created in mind, in process of becoming real
Brown: Practical
column: Strength and support.
comb: Ordered living.
commune: To bring together.
compass: Guide.
cone: Flow of energy from a higher level; to bring into reality.
copper: See "metal."
correspondence: Communication between levels of the mind.
costume: Putting on an act or concealing truth.
court: Justice; fulfilling the Law of Cause and Effect.
cow: Mother symbol; nourisher and support.
cremation: Destruction to make way for the new.
crest: Thought and beliefs related to upbringing and family.
crevice: The unknown; the subconscious mind.
crisis: Turning point; movement begins toward the opposite pole (illness to health, old to new, etc.).
crocodile: Misguided energy.

cross: Sacrifice.
crow: Messenger of new or creative beginnings.
crowd (moving): Movement of the unconscious.
crowd (fixed): Fixed beliefs.
crown: To rise to the highest.
crucifixion: Sacrifice.
crutch: Support and assistance.
cry: Emotional release.
crystal: Spirit. Also see "gem."
cube: Universe of duality, where world is perceived as opposites.
cup: Receptacle holding unlimited potential.
curtain: Veil that prevents understanding.
cycle: Repeating movement, having only the appearance of change.
dam: To stop the flow of energy.
dance: The act of creation.
darkness: Cannot see truth; trapped due to lack of understanding.
daughter: A more alive and simplistic part of self.
death: Climax or completion; sacrifice for change.
decay: A slow ending.
deep: See "inner."
degree: Level of understanding. The higher the degree, the greater the understanding.
demon: See "devil."
dependent: Avoiding responsibility.
desert: Transformations without distractions.
design: Idea; a creation in mind and not yet a reality.
destruction: Sacrificial ending.
detour: Distraction off the path being followed.
devil: One who uses universal law for his own personal gain.

dew: A whisper of a spiritual realization.
diamond: See "gem."
diary: See "book."
dictator: Restricting freedom.
diet: Restricting available energy.
different: To deny unity and similarities.
digestion: Assimilation of energy.
dimension: Level of awareness. Higher level indicates more refined awareness.
direction: Source of goodness.
  North: God or source
  East: Hierarch or elder brother; guide
  South: Mankind
  West: Self
dirty: See "filthy."
disaster: See "catastrophe."
disease: Unable to release a problem; being tense. (See Chapter 6.)
disguise: Hiding one's true intentions.
dismemberment: To remove a distraction from one's life. Also see "body". (Also see Chapter 6.)
doctor: See "occupation."
document: See "book."
dog: Faithfulness and guardian.
doll: Placing the blame on others.
dolphin: Salvation.
donkey: Stubborn; humility and patience.
door: Opening to move beyond limitations.
dot: See "center."
dove: Peace; soul.
dragon: Self-healing energy.
draw: To conceive a new plan or idea.

dream: Vision that is about to become a reality.

drift: To flow down life's stream without deep concerns.

drive: To take responsibility for one's life.

drugs: Avoidance of problems by masking symptoms.

drum: Rhythm of movement.

dummy: Primitive beliefs.

dune: See "hill."

dungeon: See "basement."

dwarf: Ignorance of man.

eagle: Spiritual ascent.

ear of corn: Fertility; germination and growth.

Earth: See "planets."

east: See "direction."

eat: To gain life energy.

echo: Fulfillment of the law of cause and effect; what is given out is received.

edge: Point of decision.

educate: To evacuate or remove false beliefs. (Also see Chapter 6.)

eel: See "serpent."

egg: Seed and source; potential for growth.

eight: See "number."

electrician: See "occupation."

electricity: Creative energy.

elephant: Strength and pity.

emerald: See "gem."

emperor: See "king."

empty: State just before fulfillment.

enchantment: Deluded and unable to see reality.

enclosure: Limitations of the self.

end: Completion of a cycle.

enemy: Opposing beliefs.

engineer: See "occupation."

entanglement: Bonds with others that distract from true mission.

entrance: See "hole."

equator: Middle path, without extremes.

erase: To hide an error.

error: A lesson to be learned.

excrement: Inner cleansing.

expert: Fixed, having little ability to learn.

eye: To see clearly; transition point. Also see "body."

fall: Move from the spiritual to the material world.

falling (sensation when waking from sleep): Consciousness returning to body. (See Chapter 6.)

falls (waterfalls): See "rain."

family: Unity.

fan: To cause spiritual movement.

farmer: Nourisher of many; teacher.

fashion: See "costume."

fastener: That which holds things as they were. Maintains status quo.

fate: Eventual outcome.

father: Morality; restraining instinct.

favor: A blessing.

feather: Ability to rise above.

fertilizer: See "manure."

field: Limitless potential.

fight: Inner conflict. (See Chapter 6.)

figure: Body of self (physical identification).

file: To smooth and refine through conflict.

filthy: Selfish.

fire: Energy of spiritual transformation.

fireplace: Home.

fish: Psychic power of the unconscious; belief.

fisherman: See "occupation."

fishing: Getting information from the unconscious.

five: See "number."

flag: Victory.

flame: See "fire."

flight: See "flying."

flocks: Yielding to force; no individuality.

flood: Spiritual cleansing. (See Chapter 6.)

flower: Process of change, transition, or growth.

flute: Distraction from the path.

flying: Rising above limitations through use of imagination. (See Chapter 6.)

fog: See "cloud."

food: Source of energy.

fool: Idiot or genius. See "genius."

foot: See "body."

footprints: The way left by those before; the path.

footwear: Protection along the path of life.

force: Universal energy.

forest: Peace and quiet.

fork: A point of decision.

fossil: Eternal.

fountain: Life force. Source of goodness.

four: See "number."

fox: Slyness.

fracture: Separation. (See Chapter 6.)

freeze: To become hard and fixed, unable to adapt.

friction: To learn through conflict.

friend: different aspects of self.

fruit: Source of energy.

fuel: Source of energy.

fulcrum: Aid in work.

funnel: See "cone."

fur: Nature of animal energy (finer hair = more refined nature).

furniture: Personality.

game: Life.

garden: Unlimited potential for growth.

garland: Celebration.

gem: Catalyst or spiritual keys.
   Amethyst: Healing and meditative
   Crystal: Like a diamond, but not as powerful
   Diamond: Infinite possibilities
   Emerald: Healing
   Jade: Immortality
   Lapis: Higher knowledge
   Opal: Powerful changes
   Pearl: Calm and creative
   Ruby: Knowledge
   Sapphire: Intellect
   Topaz: Logic and reason

Gemini: Person concerned with reason and logic.

genitals: See "body."

genius: One in touch with the creator.

ghost: See "spirit."

giant: Power and strength.

gift: A blessing.

gland: Energy transformers in the body.

glass: To be able to see beyond or through limitations.

gloves: Deception. Removal of gloves discloses real intentions.

glue: Emotional ties.

goal: Limited foresight on the chosen path.

gold: Superior, glorified. Also see "metal."

grafting: Forcing the natural order.

grain: See "seed."

grandparents: Loving guardians.

grapes: Fertility and sacrifice.

grass: To give way or bend.
grave: See "cemetery."
green: See "color."
guides: High beings providing inner guidance.
gun: Power outside of self.
hair: See "body."
half: Unbalanced.
hall (large room): Person having tremendous potential for improvement.
hall (narrow corridor): Person has limited choices.
hammer: Power to create.
hands: See "body."
harbor: Protection from emotional times.
hare: See "rabbit."
harp: Bridge to higher levels of mind.
harvest: Completion of the Law of Cause and Effect.
hat: Limited thinking.
head: See "body."
heal: To return to balance.
heart: Love, the center of development.
hearth: See "fireplace."
heat: Energy and growth.
heaven: Higher plateau; inner peace.
hedge: See "boundary."
height: Higher the level, higher the understanding and knowledge.
hell: Fixed living, without any growth; trapped within self-imposed boundaries.
helmet: Mental protection; having a visor indicates one is trying to hide inner feelings and thoughts.
herbs: Natural forces.
hierarch: High being that guides mankind; the white brotherhood.

hill: Small aspiration. Also see "mountain."
hippopotamus: Strength and fertility.
hog: See "pig."
hole: Fertility; opening to other worlds/levels.
home: Back to the source of truth and self.
honey: Healing energy. Energy of change.
hood: To hide true motives.
hop: Making progress.
horn (from an animal): Strength and power.
horse: Determined effort.
hourglass: Flow of goodness from the source.
house: See "building."
hunger: State of realizing the futility of present efforts, while inwardly being aware of the true potential of life.
hunter: Insatiable desires.
hurricane: Going in circles and not solving the real problem.
ice: Cold and rigid (not flexible).
idea: Creation from the source.
idiot: See "fool."
idol: Material distraction.
illness: See "disease."
imagination: To create in mind.
incest: To unite with the essence of one's true self (soul).
indigestion: Going against the flow of life or the natural flow of energy.
inheritance: Gains made through past action.
injury: To call attention to. (See Chapter 6.)
inner: The essence or true nature of.
insane: See "fool."
instrument: Assistance in accomplishing task.

intercourse (sexual): To unify male and female polarities within the self.

inversion: Reversal of state (death to birth, sorrow to joy, old to new, etc.).

invisible: Repressed.

iron: Inflexible and unyielding. Also see "metal."

ivy: Need for protection.

jade: See "gem."

jealous: Vigilant in guarding a possession.

jewel: See "gem."

job: Role or duty.

journey: A search for truth.

judge: See "occupation."

juice: Life-giving energy source.

jungle: Confused thoughts.

Jupiter: See "planets."

key: On the threshold of a solution.

kill: To destroy the old to prepare the way for the new.

king: Idealized self.

kiss: Pure love.

knife: See "sword."

knight: Chivalry and protection.

knot: Restriction.

knowledge: Inner wisdom.

Krishna: High being teaching duty and devotion.

labyrinth: Lost and confused.

lack: Looking for goodness in the wrong direction.

ladder: See "steps."

lake: Mirror of the soul; transition plane to different levels of consciousness.

lamb: Innocence and sacrifice.

lamp: To illuminate the way.

lance: Sacrificial staff. Also see "staff."

lane: See "path."

lapis: See "gem."

last: Holding on, resisting change.

laugh: Releasing tension.

laurel: Victory.

lavatory: Place and time for inner cleansing.

law: Truth.

lawyer: See "occupation."

leaf: Happiness.

learn: Unfoldment of truth; to remove hang-ups.

leech: To be dependent and deny one's own abilities.

left: Feminine; intuitive.

leg: See "body."

Leo: Person concerned with leadership.

leopard: Aggressiveness.

letter (document): Guidance.

letter: Similar to "number."

  A,J,S: = 1 = Unity, source

  B,K,T: = 2 = Duality, seeking balance, creation

  C,L,U: = 3 = Trinity, strength

  D,M,V: = 4 = Fixed, able to manifest

  E,N,W: = 5 = Emotional, creative

  F,O,X: = 6 = Healing

  G,P,Y: = 7 = Change, growth

  H,Q,Z: = 8 = Completion, to higher balance

  I,R: = 9 = Celebration

level: Balanced.

Libra: Person concerned with balancing events.

library: place to hold records.

license: To work within the letter of the law but not necessarily holding to the spirit of the law.

life: Aliveness.

light: Illumination; to shine the way; to see clearly.

lightning: Great energy.

lily: Purity.

limit: Boundary created by the mind.

link: See "key."

lion: Latent passion.
list: See "book."
load: Responsibility for past actions.
lock: Restrictions.
locust: Destruction that allows for new growth.
look: To see, usually without understanding.
loop: See "circle."
loss: Removal to open the way for something new.
lotus: Unfoldment to higher awareness or truth.
love: Unity.
lungs: See "body."
lure: Distractions off the path being followed.
machine: Repetitious movement; doing without thinking.
magician: One who makes changes within universal laws.
man: Active nature of the self.
mandala (symbol): Symbolic representation of a mantra (chant).
manna: Energy from the source.
manure: Trash that can become useful if properly utilized.
manuscript: See "book."
map: Guide showing path.
march: Those who exist without growth or change.
market: Ability to choose from many sources.
marriage: Unity; to become one.
Mars: See "planets."
marsh: See "swamp."
martyr: See "sacrifice."
mask: An act to hide one's true intentions.
mason: See "occupation."
massage: Rebalancing of the body.
master: High being to teach those who are ready.
masturbation: Fooling self.
math: The order of things.

meadow: Peace within.
meat: Animal desires.
medicine: See "drugs."
meditation: To become silent.
melody: The rhythm of universal movements.
memory: Past lessons repeated.
Mercury: See "planets."
mercy: Attempt to go around the Law.
message: Guidance.
metal:
  Aluminum: Feasibility and flexibility
  Chrome: Preservation of appearances
  Copper: Conductor of energy; emotional protection
  Gold: Spiritual attainment and oneness
  Iron and steel: Strength and rigidity
  Silver: Source of energy
meteor: About to be born.
mind: The ability to create.
mirage: To experience and not see the truth of what happened.
mirror: Seeing only the image and not the real truth.
mission: Lesson to be learned.
mist: Prevents seeing truth.
mob: Action without thought.
mold: Continuing the same pattern.
mole: To move in the dark, without understanding.
molt: To remove obvious animal characteristics.
money: Greed.
monk: Self-denial.
monkey: Unconscious desires.
monocle: Third eye (located in middle of forehead). Allows one to see more clearly.
monsoon: See "rain."
monster: Revealing lower aspects of self.

moon: An emotional event; intuition. Also see "planets."

moral: Inner battle between right and wrong.

moth: Natural attraction to light.

mother: Nourisher, protective instinct.

motion: To take action.

mountain: High aspirations.

mouth: See "body."

movie: See "theater."

mud: Plasticity. Easily molded and changed.

mug: See "cup."

mummy: To preserve the outer appearance.

murder: Self-destruction.

music: Higher universal form of communication.

mystic: Illumined teacher.

name: Characteristics of.

nature: The order of things; freedom.

navy: See "armed forces."

neck: See "body."

necklace: Restriction. If tight, restricting will. If loose, restricting love.

negative: To remove.

Neptune: See "planets."

nerve: To feel.

nest: See "home."

net: Entanglement and traps. Also see "web."

new: Change.

night: What is seen has not yet become a reality.

nine: See "number."

noise: Confusion.

nomad: Searcher. Looking for direction.

north: See "direction."

note: See "message."

nude: In the process of changing personality.

number: Similar to "letter."

1 = Unity, source, Christ, channel

2 = Duality, seeking balance, creation

3 = Trinity, balanced, strength

4 = Fixed, able to manifest

5 = Emotional, creative

6 = Healing

7 = Change, growth

8 = Completion, higher balance

9 = mental completion, celebration

0 = Total completion; beyond cyclic changes

oar: Assistance.

oasis: Salvation.

occupation: Type of service.

Actor: Playing a role

Architect: Redesigning etheric (blueprint) body

Artist: Creating or building the new

Butcher: Destroying animal instincts

Carpenter: Rebuilding body

Chef: Providing energy to the body

Clerk: Keeping record of accomplishments and mistakes

Doctor: Etheric (blueprint of the body) healer

Electrician: Rebuilding nervous system

Engineer: Becoming aware of different levels and making them work in unison

Fisherman: In search of higher beliefs

Judge: Maintaining the natural order

Lawyer: Studying the natural order of things

Mason: Increasing body's

strength and tolerance to external turmoil

Painter (house): Protecting the body

Philosopher: Unifying differences

Plumber: Rebuilding gastrointestinal system

Professor: Teaching from a higher level

Secretary: Assistance in accomplishing goals

Supervisor: Regaining control of the different aspects of one's own life

ocean: Dynamic forces (rough = problems; calm = serenity).

octave: Expression within a single level of awareness; working within the known or existing system.

octopus: Unfolding of a process.

oil: Help to ease completion of a task or job.

old: Low in energy. About to come to an end.

olive tree: Peace.

one: See "number."

opal: See "gem."

opening: See "hole."

orange: See "color."

order: See "law."

organ (musical instrument): Religion.

oven: Giver of energy.

owl: Passive attitude.

ox: Self-sacrifice.

paddle: See "oar."

painter: See "occupation."

painting: Process of building or creating.

parade: Premature celebration.

parallel: Continue along a seemingly different path, leading to the same goal.

party: Celebration of completion.

passage: See "hole."

paste: See "glue."

path: Guided journey.

peacock: Blending or unifying the many into the one.

pearl: Hidden genius; heaven. Also see "gem."

Pegasus: To change evil into good; to rise above.

pen or pencil: Capability of recording past deeds for easy access.

people: See "mob."

pepper: To add excitement through irritation.

perfect: Observation from a higher level; to see good in all.

perfume: Memories.

phallus: Perpetuation of life.

philosopher: See "occupation."

phoenix: Regeneration of life.

pickle: To preserve.

picture: See "painting."

pig: To indulge material or earthly desires.

pilgrim: One who ventures forth.

pillow: Mental support.

pin: See "fastener."

pine: Fertility.

Pisces: Person concerned with beliefs.

planets: Forces of change.

  Mercury: Mind and communication

  Venus: Love and beauty

  Earth: Mother and nourisher

  Moon: Imagination and feelings

  Mars: Activity and action

  Jupiter: Plenty and fortune

  Saturn: Life work and the wholeness of life

  Uranus: Unexpected happenings

  Neptune: Spirituality and the unconscious

Pluto: Institutions and karma (Law of Cause and Effect)
plant: Adaptability.
plastic: Capable of being molded.
play: To enjoy.
pleasure: Sensual gratification of desires.
plough: See "till."
plumber: See "occupation."
Pluto: See "planet."
pocket: To conceal; to hold.
point: Source.
pole: Spirituality.
police: Keeper of the order.
politics: Immoral behavior, where the end justifies the means.
pond: See "lake".
pool: See "lake."
porpoise: See "dolphin."
port: See "harbor."
positive: To increase.
pot: To contain or limit.
potion: Key to changes.
powder (cosmetic): See "mask."
power: Desire to control.
pray: To search for answers from someone other than self.
president: Political head. Also see "politics."
prince: A change for the better in male identity.
princess: A change for the better in female identity.
procession: Having domination over whatever is carried.
professor: See "occupation."
program: No vitality in life; following the script.
project: Planned action.
proof: Inner realization.
psyche: Soul.
psychic: One who is consciously in contact with the soul.
purple: See "color."
putty: Easily molded.

pyramid: Rebirth and immortality; balanced.
quality: Attribute or level of awareness.
quantity: Materialistic.
queen: Idealized self.
question: To search for an answer.
rabbit: To increase quickly.
radical: One who is frustrated with one extreme and proposes the other extreme.
radio: See "telephone."
rags: Remnants of old personality.
rain: Purification.
rainbow: A blessing.
ranch: See "farm."
rape: To destroy innocence.
rat: Death.
reality: Perceived truth, subject to change with time.
reason: Excuse.
rebel: See "radical."
recognize: To see oneself.
record: See "book."
red: See "color."
reef: Emotional protection.
reins: Self-control or will power.
residue: Essence of.
resonance: To become attuned to.
restaurant: Many sources of energy and help.
return: To repent and forgive oneself.
revolution: To change direction, taking a different path.
rhythm: Moving to the universal drummer; doing what is best in spite of outer pressures.
rib: See "seed."
right: Masculine; active.
ring: Continuity and wholeness.
riot: See "mob."
rise: To see from a level of greater understanding and intelligence.

rites: Ceremony for creation. The process of bringing into existence.

river: Channel that allows movement through life with minimal conflict; source of life.

road: See "path."

rock: Permanence and harmony.

rod: Higher thoughts, channeled in from a higher level.

roof: Limits of thinking.

room: Physical self.

rooster: Activity.

root: Foundation.

rope: Ability to go beyond restrictions.

rose (flower): Unfoldment; perfection and completion when completely open.

rot: See "decay."

rotation: See "cycle."

royalty: In service of the higher forces.

rubber: Ability to try again.

ruby: See "gem."

rudder: In control of.

ruin: Destruction over a long period of time; an ending of the old.

rule: See "law."

run: Changes in self. (See Chapter 6.)

rust: See "decay."

sack: See "basket."

sacrifice: Highest form of love.

saddle: To weigh down, restrict.

safe: See "vault."

Sagittarius: Person concerned with reality.

sail: Creative spirit.

saint: Illumined teacher.

salt: To preserve.

salute: To acknowledge.

sample: To play with, without getting deeply involved.

sand: Endless and eternal.

sandal: See "footwear."

sapphire: See "gem."

Saturn: See "planets."

scales: Balance; justice.

scar: Hates and bad memories.

scarf: See "flag."

scent: A recognizable quality from the past.

scepter: See "staff."

schedule: A personal timetable.

school: Place of learning. (See Chapter 6.)

science: The study of relationships.

score: Tally of past actions. Greater the score for self, greater the debt owed to others. Greater the score for others, greater the debt repaid.

Scorpio: Person concerned with creating.

scrap (leftover): Sin of omission (things not completed).

scream: To call attention to.

screen (as for a window): Goal that is just out of reach.

scribe: Recording of past deeds.

scythe: To reap or harvest. Results of past actions.

sea: See "ocean."

season: Life of man.
   Spring: Birth, beginnings
   Summer: Growth, learning
   Autumn: Maturity, teaching
   Winter: Death, ending

secret: Keys for releasing love, light, and power.

section: Focusing on one part, and therefore unable to see the whole.

seed: Latent forces; about to come into reality.

sense: To feel.

sentry: Obstacle to goal.

service: To work off past debts (owed for misdeeds).

seven: See "number."

sex: See "intercourse."

shade: Unable to clearly see the truth.

shadow: A hint of the new personality that is coming into being.

shoe: See "footwear."

sign: Characteristic of.

six: See "number."

slave: Tied into situations of life.

sleep: To rest and revitalize both body and mind.

smell: The attribute or characteristic of.

smoke: Unable to see clearly; protection.

smooth: Without difficulty.

snake: Healing energy; source of knowledge and inner wisdom.

snorkel: Having mental clarity during an emotional event.

snow: To become new or purified again.

soap: Purification and cleansing.

solar plexus: See "body."

soldier: One whose life is controlled and sacrificed by others.

son: A more alive and simplistic part of self.

sound: Energy.

south: See "direction."

space: Silence; existence between states or levels.

spark: A beginning.

spear: See "staff."

sphere: See "circle."

spice: To conceal the true nature of.

spin: To have movement without any real progress.

spine: See "body."

spirit: The essence of life.

splint: Support.

sport: To bring mind and body into harmony.

spot: See "center."

spring: See "season."

spur: To urge into action.

square: Lack of balance, unyeilding.

squirrel: Preparation for the future.

stable: See "barn."

staff: Mystical channel to higher truth; wisdom.

stage: See "theater."

stains: Changes.

star: Guidance.

starch: Rigid and unchanging.

static: Without growth; no real change.

statue: Self.

steel: See "metal."

steep: Shorter but more difficult path.

steps: Channel to rise (idealism) or decline (practicality).

stitch: To make whole again.

stomach: See "body."

stone: See "rock."

store: Unlimited potential.

storm: Period of emotional cleansing.

story: Belief.

stranger: Lost person; no direction in life.

straw: See "grass."

stream: Emotional cleanser.

street: See "path."

stress: Inner conflict between choices.

student: One in search of truth.

study: Search for truth.

style: See "personality."

substitute: To replace with another having similar outer appearance, but inwardly is completely different.

suffer: Inability to reach a goal.

summer: See "season."

summit: Highest aspirations.

summons: An inner calling.

sun: Source of energy.

sunrise or sunset: Emotional energy used for healing.
supervisor: See "occupation."
supporters: Guides or angels; helpers.
swamp: Emotional confusion.
sweep: To clear or remove a past debt.
swimming: Emotional cleansing.
swivel: See "spin."
sword: Sacrifice. Also see "cross."
symbols: Characteristics of.
symptom: Outward manifestation of an inner movement.
table: Elevation.
table (round): Equality.
tablet: See "book."
tadpole: Undergoing emotional changes.
tail: Repressed animalistic characteristics.
tailbone: See "body."
talk: Communication; to give life to thoughts.
target: See "goal."
Taurus: Person concerned with acquisitions.
tax: Price for whatever is attained.
teacher: See "occupation."
teeth: See "body."
telephone: Aid in communication; to project over large distances.
telescope: Aid in seeing clearly.
television: See "theater."
tent: See "canopy."
tetrahedron: Balance of physical, emotional, mental, and spiritual aspects.
theater: Playing a role.
theft: To obtain what has not been earned.
theory: A guess.
thermometer: A measure of warmth and love. Warmer the temperature, the greater the warmth and love.
thirst: Desire for inner emotional cleansing.
thorn: Pain to initiate change. Pain brings awareness, which makes change possible.
thought: Process of reason and logic.
thread: Connection between different levels or planes of awareness.
three: See "number."
thresh: Getting to the source or core.
throne: Inherited position and support.
tides: Emotional movement, not to be denied.
tiger: Wrath and cruelty.
till: Preparation for growth.
timber: Material for support.
time: Periodic movement within cycles.
  Past: Memories
  Present: Now
  Future: Dreams and desires
title: Theme; summary.
toilet: Time and place for inner cleansing.
toll: Payment for whatever is obtained.
tomb: An ending. Whatever is in tomb will end to open way for something new. If self in tomb, personality is about to change.
tone: Call to a level of awareness.
tool: Aid or assistance.
top: See "summit."
topaz: See "gem."
torch: Light to shine the way.
tortoise: Long life.
total: In touch with all aspects of self.

tower: To rise above.
toy: Temptation from the past.
tradition: Tied to the past.
trail: See "path."
transportation: Rapid progress or change.
trap: To limit yourself.
trash: Destruction of the old.
travel: To view from another's viewpoint.
treasure: Gains made in life.
tree: Inexhaustible life.
trespass: To venture beyond the known.
trial: To measure the debt.
triangle: Strength and stability.
trigger: Key to movement and progress.
trim: Removing excess.
trip: Done over a long period of time.
triumph: Completion.
tropical: Increased energy.
trumpet: Desire for fame and glory.
truth: Unmoving, unchanging state of reality.
tumor: See "cancer (disease)."
tune: To move in harmony with.
tunnel: Moving into a new life or level of awareness.
turban: See "hat."
turkey: Stupid.
turtle: Long life.
twin: Same attributes.
twist: Movement in circles.
two: See "number."
typhoon: See "hurricane."
tyrant: Restricting life; not moving with the flow of life.
ulcer: Inner drive for growth that is not being realized; inner restrictions.
umbrella: See "canopy."
unicorn: Innocence and purity.
unlock: To release.

unmask: To see into the deeper nature of the self.
Uranus: See "planets."
urine: Inner cleansing.
used: Repetition of action.
vacation: To vacate or empty self.
vacuum: Alone, in silence.
valley: See "crevice."
vampire: Animalistic desires.
vault: Protection during change.
vegetation: Abundance; change in progress for the better.
vehicle: Assistance in movement; may be own body.
veil: Illusion, unable to see clearly.
Venus: Love and beauty.
vessel: Container or limits.
vibration: Feelings.
victory: Completion of struggle.
vine: See "rope."
violet: See "color."
virgin: Innocence.
Virgo: Person concerned with organization.
voice: Inner guidance.
volcano: Inner drive to seek a spiritual life.
vulture: Help in process of change.
wait: Period before change when nothing appears to be happening.
wall: Limitations.
wand: See "staff."
war: Inner conflict or struggle.
warmth: Energy and comfort.
warrior: Latent forces to aid in conflict.
wash: See "bath."
waste: Elimination of negative.
water: Emotional consciousness.
waves: Purification.
way: See "path."
weak: Easily distracted.

web: Mental confusion with the complexity of life.
weeds: Haphazard growth.
weep: To feel sorry for self.
well: Salvation.
west: See "direction."
wheel: Cycles; repeating events.
whip: Punishment and domination.
white: See "color."
whole: Completion.
wide: Having many possibilities.
wild: Freedom.
win: Continuing with the same pattern of life.
wind: Strong thoughts; energy.
window: To see beyond one's limitations.
wine: Blood and sacrifice.
wing: Imagination; spirituality.
winter: See "seasons."
witch: One who works with natural forces.

witness: Soul.
woman: Passive nature.
wood: See "timber."
wool: Protection.
work: Completing task the hard way.
world: To see the overall plan, the big picture.
worm: The destroyer that opens the way for something new.
wrap: To mask, disguise, or hide.
wristwatch: Orderly, restricted living.
yang: Masculine, or active, force.
yellow: See "color."
yin: Feminine or passive force.
yoke: Discipline; union, to ease task.
young: Much energy; vital but without discipline.
zero: See "number."
zoo: See "barn."